THE RELEVANCE OF THE CHURCH

BY THE SAME AUTHOR

THE RELEVANCE OF CHRISTIANITY
(*Fifth Edition*)

THE RELEVANCE
OF THE CHURCH

BY

F. R. BARRY

M.A., D.S.O.

CANON OF WESTMINSTER
AND RECTOR OF ST. JOHN'S, SMITH SQUARE
CHAPLAIN TO THE KING

LONDON: NISBET AND CO. LTD.
22 BERNERS STREET, W. 1

First Published in 1935

Made and Printed in Great Britain

"THE SIMPLICITY THAT IS IN CHRIST."

2 *Cor. xi. 3.*

"IN RELIGIOUS PROBLEMS, SIMPLE SOLUTIONS ARE BOGUS SOLUTIONS."

—*Whitehead.*

The Moorhouse Lectures, which furnish much of the material for this book, were delivered in St. Paul's Cathedral, Melbourne, during November, 1934.

CONTENTS

CHAPTER VI

INTRODUCTION

"THEY must have a Church," said the Duke of Wellington, in appointing William Grant Broughton to the archdeaconry of New South Wales.[1] Nonchalance or prophetic vision, it is due in great measure to the Duke's insistence and to the courage, insight and tenacity of the great man whom he chose to nominate, that the Church had the right to take part in the Melbourne centenary of last year.

It did this on a most ambitious scale. In connection with the official celebrations, the Archbishop of Melbourne arranged a congress, at which there were present Bishops and others from nearly every diocese in the continent, for the re-affirmation of the Gospel which the Church offers to Australia. The Moorhouse Lectures, on which this book is based, were delivered in the course of this congress at the invitation of the Archbishop. What hidden depths there must be in a people which is willing to include a series of lectures in a programme of national festivity ! It was a great honour for me to be asked to take part in this commemoration. I cannot adequately express my gratitude for the education which the experience gave me. Nor can my wife or I ever forget the overwhelming kindness extended to us, both per-

---

[1] Archdeacon of N.S.W., 1829, first Bishop of Australia, 1836, Metropolitan of Sydney, 1847.

sonally and officially, during our visit to the Australian
Church.

The centenary proclaimed to the world the amazing
enterprise and vitality which seem to be in the blood
of our race. But what has bred the greatness of
Britain is, before all else, its Christianity. The Church
welded it into national unity and first taught it the
uses of self-government. The Church fed its passion
for freedom as against privilege and usurpation, and
championed the liberties of the common man. The
Church gave it liberal education and the discipline
of the Christian tradition. Whatever we owe to
climate and geography, to fortune or to inborn char-
acteristics, it is Christian inspiration and leadership
which have been decisive in our inheritance.

Australia was born from that spiritual parentage.
The Church has sustained, steadied and instructed it
through the period of tumultuous adolescence, growing to maturity in its growth. The Nation now
stands at the open gateway of the next stage in
historical development. It was well to pause beside
this milestone, at the perilous cross-roads of modern
history, to ask the place of the Christian religion,
especially the Anglican interpretation of it, in the
future not only of Australia, but of the whole Commonwealth of British peoples.

The nations are moving towards a new era at
present unforeseen and unpredictable ; and the
world in which the Church must now live cannot be
even approximately the same as the world of the
founders and pioneers. So incredibly fast are we
moving that in popular usage the word Victorian is

now almost a synonym for primitive. A generation is now taking control for whom " pre-war " means almost prehistoric. Was the religion which we have inherited so inextricably interwoven with the pattern of thought, emotion and conduct which ruled nine-teenth-century society that it cannot survive its dis-integration ? Or does it contain within itself such vital and creative resources that it may lead us into a new future amid tasks, conditions and opportunities undreamed of yet in our philosophy ?

The greatest triumphs of our religion in the hundred years that are now closing have been overseas and in the mission-field. There the Churches, confronted with obstacles and with a lack of man-power and resources which we would have found daunting, if not fatal, have achieved a record of enterprise and courage which may well put the Home Church to shame. If we would estimate its vitality, we should study the Church in the British Dominions and in those new nations stepping into history under Christian guidance and tutelage. There can be no doubt about the answer : Christianity is woven into the texture of all that is noblest in our traditions. We have only to think of the faith and courage which have gone to the building up of great nations, trans-planting all that is best in our inheritance into new conditions in far distant countries—and then to separate that, if we can, from the legacy of Christian conviction. Whatever is best and most fundamental in us we owe to our ancestral Christianity ; whatever we can contribute to the future is inalienably dependent on it.

And it is scarcely possible to exaggerate what the world has yet the right to expect of us. What we have seen in Europe in the last decade has revealed the spiritual sterility of self-contained economic nationalism resting only on secular foundations. We have learnt something of its intrinsic horror. It appears to us to violate everything that British tradition holds most in reverence. A secularised nationalist policy unredeemed by spiritual conviction not only starves a people's soul : it will also bring with it physical starvation. For no appearance of economic revival can be other than illusory and short-lived till we have solved the international problem. Statesmen who promise anything else delude us. Nor can we remember too often that our English inheritance of liberty, which we prize even above life itself, is bound up with our English Christianity. Faith and Freedom go together. Where Faith dies, Freedom perishes. It is happening all over the world to-day.

The demoralisation of Europe is the wasting fever of a lost faith. There can be no hope for the revival of international co-operation or of free, liberal institutions except upon a spiritual foundation. We cannot look to the future with confidence, apart from the contribution of Christianity in sustaining the spiritual values of national and international life. The leadership of Europe is still ours, if we have the courage and insight to assume it. Yet without some ultimate conviction we shall be but blind guides leading blind men. We can take our true place in Europe only if we can stand forth as a Christian nation.

But Europe is only a small part of the world, and the great decisions no longer rest in the hands of Europeans alone. New influences have entered the field of force. For example, the delicate and dangerous issues of pacts on the eastern frontier of Germany are inseparable from Far Eastern politics. The centres of gravity are shifting from the Atlantic to the Pacific basin, and the fate of Western Europe is bound up with the success or failure of the Churches in the Christianisation of the Far East. Thus it needs but little imagination to envisage the great tasks of leadership which are reserved for the Australian people as the chief Christian power of the Pacific. It is not too much to say that the whole future depends on the depth, reality and effectiveness of our English-speaking Christianity.

Once more, to take a totally different area, we may think of the Anglo-Egyptian Sudan. One can hardly believe that in less than forty years, since the end of the Mahdist *régime*, British rule could have achieved so much. Tribes who have been, since the Pharaohs, the victims of iniquitous exploitation are being led to the gateways of nationhood. The sterile blight of massacre and the slave-trade is being redeemed into fruitful enterprise and constructive education for freedom. It is one of the brightest pages in our record. But all this disinterested service has been, and is, confessedly inspired by the consecrations of Christian loyalty.

The study of history during the last century leaves no room for doubt that the Christian faith is the great formative force that holds the future. But if it can

do so much in its weakness, in the sorry caricature
that we have made of it, what may it not do in its
strength and its reality ?

Faced with so many incalculable forces as those
which bewilder and frighten the world to-day, the
tendency of the pre-war generations is to revert to a
mere traditionalism. Of this the young are properly
impatient. They wish to break free into a new era,
and are rightly suspicious of any programme which
seems to suggest a reversion to the past. Christianity
too suffers from this suspicion. It will never com-
mend itself to the young or claim their still uncom-
mitted loyalties if it is presented as a mere plea for
the resuscitation of the past or the artificial recovery
of a tradition. This seems to me to be a right attitude.
The spirit of Christ is essentially creative, and must
embody itself in new forms with the changing needs
of changing generations. The wine of its inexhaustible
resources must continually be poured into new bottles.
But the Anglican interpretation of the faith bequeathed
to us by our predecessors appears to be uniquely
adapted to meet the religious needs of the present
age.

For the genius of the Anglican inheritance is
experiment working upon tradition. We no longer
suppose, like Dr. Thwackum, that Christianity always
and everywhere means the English Act of Uniformity,
or sung matins and litany at eleven. Neither in a
social nor a religious heritage is there such a thing as a
fresh start—for the life of Christ's Church is continuous ; and the building into Melbourne Cathedral
of a stone from Westminster Abbey was a happy

symbol of that continuity. But there is such a thing
as creative evolution. And it is the glory of the English Church to have been instructed as the householder,
bringing out of its treasures things both new and old.
The householder metaphor is pregnant. For, in the
words of the last Lambeth Conference, " Every
Church of our communion is endeavouring to do for
the country where it exists the service that the Church
of England has done for England—to represent the
Christian religion and the catholic faith in a manner
congenial to the people of the land, and to give scope
to their genius in the development of Christian life
and worship." [1] It would be a disaster if the overseas Churches were to reproduce in distant continents
the controversies and the limitations which have been
imposed on the Church in England by the accidents
of European history. Anglicanism is something
far richer and more flexible than Church-of-
Englandism.

There are two policies now before the Church.
By way of illustrating the two alternatives, it is not
hard to think of two dioceses in different parts of the
Anglican Communion. In one, our Church has
taken its stand stiffly on the strictest formularies of
Churchmanship. Its membership consists of the
clergy and a small inner circle of the devout, while
the great mass of the laity are outside. In the other,
it is functioning as the conscience of the whole
English-speaking community, and supplying the
leadership and inspiration of all its moral and religious
ideals. The official policy of the latter diocese would

[1] Lambeth *Encyclical*, 1930, p. 29.

be censured in the former as laxity. But which of the two has understood best the true and authentic Anglican tradition ?

The Church of England has never been a sect. When most vital and most true to itself it has been the soul and conscience of the nation ; and it may be claimed that at the present moment, after years of comparative eclipse, it has regained the chance to discharge this function. Its spokesmen are once more the acknowledged leaders of Christian opinion in matters of public policy.

It may be still deplorably out of touch with the great majority of our population. But it has before it an opportunity greater than any that has yet been offered to us. In the bankruptcy of secular leadership, our people are willing, and even eager, to accept a strong lead from their Church. It need give but a few generous gestures, and the people of England will be with it. But if Anglicanism fails the world now, it is no other form of Christianity which will win its allegiance, but paganism.

In the following chapters I make some attempt to estimate the existing opportunity, and to inquire how we may best meet it. I have tried to appraise the contemporary reaction against institutional religion, and to suggest the true line of approach to reviving the idea of the Church in its relevance to the world situation. Next, I endeavour to set forth the theology on which such an enterprise must depend, and to follow out some of its implications into the sphere of Christian public worship, the ethical content of the Christian life, and the function of the Christian society in its widest and most catholic ideal, as the Body of Christ in the world.

My last book was received with a kindness which was almost embarrassingly generous, and brought me many new friends and great encouragement. It was, however, exposed to the just criticism of leaving the reader too much in the air. The question " Exactly what does this book mean ? " must have been singularly hard to answer. I have wished for some time to remedy the defect. Not long after that book was published, I met in Oxford a well-known divine, who observed " That task was comparatively easy ; what you have to do next is much more difficult—to explain what is the relevance of the Church."

It was that remark which produced the present volume. For several years I have cherished the hope of trying to show how the main arguments which had been developed in the earlier book could be applied to the actual conditions of the Churches as they exist in the world to-day. The invitation to lecture in Australia supplied the occasion for making the attempt.

It had been my intention to include a good deal more than what is now published. In particular, I had projected a chapter which was to discuss some very topical questions in regard to the organisation of the Church, and to ask how far the existing systems, whether administrative or financial, whether in the parishes or at the centre, really serve the Church's true end as an education in Christian faith and practice. This would, I think, have materially

B

increased the interest and solidity of the book. But pressure of work after my return has made this idea quite impracticable, and I was compelled reluctantly to abandon it. Those who undertake the *rôle* of Issachar (Gen. xlix. 14) must clip their literary aspirations.

This book may well seem almost parochial, alike in ambition and in achievement, when compared with the wide range of its predecessor. I can only reply that this was deliberate, and indeed essential to its immediate purpose. A great many books are now being published which discuss Christianity from out-side. My aim here has been to start from inside, from within the faith and experience of the fellow-ship centred in the parish church (or its equivalent in the Free Church polities) and thence to explore some of its implications and envisage some of its wider possibilities. This makes the treatment some-what less imaginative, but also, I venture to hope, more realistic.

Much of what follows was written, perforce, at sea. Certain traces of undulatory movement which, as I have been told, are observable in the form and matter of one section may be explained, even if not justified, by the behaviour of that capricious element. But I cannot omit a word of acknowledgement to the officers of the Orient Line for the courtesy and consideration which enabled me to do any work at all. As before, the material of these chapters was eagerly planned and debated in talk with my friend, the Bishop of Coventry. He was not able to see the final draft, but has devoted part of his convalescence to the melancholy task of proof-reading, and has helped me with many invaluable suggestions. I have also to thank my friend, L. S. Hunter, Archdeacon of Northumberland, for a like service ; my wife for constant encouragement and criticism and for laborious work with a type-writer ; and my publisher for his forbearance.

F. R. B.

WESTMINSTER,
April, 1935.

THE RELEVANCE OF THE CHURCH

CHAPTER I

THE CHRISTIAN OPPORTUNITY

1. A CENTURY OF CHURCH LIFE

THE history of the past hundred years has been not seldom misrepresented as though it were that of the last Christian century—the age when religion was slowly dying, defeated by scientific emancipation and its own interior intellectual weakness. It is the exact opposite of the truth. On the contrary, this has been the age of almost miraculous expansion. It has been one of the most creative periods. The most signal expansion of Christianity, as a great German scholar has said, belongs to the nineteenth century not the first. " The advance of Christianity in the early days was small and slow compared with its recent growth and the work of modern missions." [1] It may be briefly reviewed under four headings ; and if we think chiefly of our own Church it is not that we either forget or undervalue the precious contributions of the other Churches. The story has been so admirably told in a recent book by the Dean of Exeter [2] that we need no

[1] H. Weinel, quoted by Edwyn Bevan, *Christianity*, p. 231.
[2] *Church and People*, 1789–1889, by S. C. Carpenter (S.P.C.K.).

more here than a rapid summary. Let us take first :—

(*a*) *Missionary Expansion.* In 1835, as is now notorious, Australia was in the diocese of Calcutta—a See which had only recently been founded (1814) under pressure from Wilberforce and Simeon. ("It was," says Carpenter, " the Evangelicals who taught the Church to be missionary.") Those were, no doubt, great days for archdeacons. The Archdeacon, wrote the Secretary of State, " is to take rank and precedency in the Colony next after the Lieut.-Governor ; and you will on all public occasions be careful to confer on him such marks of attention as may most effectually recommend his person and his Sacred Office to the respect of the lower and less educated classes of society." [1] Government raised every kind of difficulty about the creation of overseas dioceses, and archdeacons flourished *sedibus vacantibus*. But the growth of the Anglican episcopate in the century with which we are now concerned may be taken as the outward, visible sign of inward and spiritual vitality. In the year 1834 there were five dioceses outside Great Britain [2] : none in the whole of Africa or Australia, one (Calcutta) for the whole of India. Australia received its first Bishop (Broughton) in 1836 ; in the present year its Church life is organised

[1] Despatch of Bathurst to Sir T. Brisbane, Dec. 21, 1824. Quoted in Giles, *Constitutional History of the Australian Church*, p. 203.

[2] Nova Scotia (1787), Quebec (1793), Calcutta (1814), Jamaica and Barbados (1824). Madras was founded in 1835, Australia (Sydney) 1836, Bombay 1837, Toronto and Newfoundland 1839, New Zealand (Auckland) 1841, Capetown, Melbourne and Newcastle 1847.

in 25 dioceses and 4 Provinces. There are today, outside the British Isles, 149 Anglican dioceses, and in the whole Anglican Communion not less than 218 Bishops.[1] Areas which but a hundred years ago were undiscovered or unoccupied or held by struggling and obscure missions—regarded either as *partes infidelium* or as parts of the diocese of London—now support great self-governing Churches under the rule of their own Metropolitans, themselves bases or " advanced headquarters " of vigorous missionary activity.

This startling movement of expansion is the constitutional and organic expression of an intense missionary development covering the whole of the earth's surface, from the tropical jungle to the frozen Labrador, which is without parallel in Christian history. Those who charge it against the English Church that it is incapable of breeding saints cannot have studied its missionary annals. There is a story of heroic sainthood, of consecrations, martyrdoms and sacrifices which are its proudest claim on our loyalties. Those who, in face of its missionary achievement in the regeneration of degraded tribesmen and the building up of new nations, still regard Christianity as a spent force, must be wilfully blinding themselves to evidence. Wherever the Gospel has been preached, the School and the Hospital have gone with it : what it did for our sodden Saxon

---

[1] This figure does not include the 103 " Protestant Episcopal " Bishops of U.S.A. in communion with the C. of E. " Bishops " here and in the text mean Diocesans, and excludes Suffragans and Coadjutors.

ancestors it has proved its power to achieve in the
redemption of Hindu Untouchables and the education of Melanesian cannibals, in the national Renaissance of Uganda, and in the Christian Universities of
the Far East. Western civilisation has inflicted foul
and ghastly wrongs on the backward peoples in its
exploitation of material wealth, and we are all in the
same condemnation. When it is cited before the
judgment of history its chief hope of a favourable
verdict lies in that which the Christian Church has
done.

In devoting itself to its proper task of evangelisation
and redemption, the English Church has found its
own life. It has learnt the meaning of fellowship in
service, both as between the various " schools of
thought " within its own ample embraces and as
between itself and the other Churches. It is in this
cooperative enterprise that the dream of a Church one
and universal has come nearest to actualisation, as
the South India project can testify. The hope of
reunion lies with the new Churches. And while our
Church has been spreading branches outwards it has
also taken root downwards. It has outgrown many
of its insular prejudices and has come to a far clearer
understanding of its place and its vocation in
Christendom.

(b) *Internal Development*. The Melbourne centenary,
during the celebrations of which these lectures were
delivered, very nearly synchronised with that of the
Oxford or Tractarian Movement. While Broughton
was journeying to England to plead for more chap-
lains in Australia to lay secure spiritual foundations

for the great national future which he foresaw, John Henry Newman was editing the Tracts. Whatever the final verdict on the Tractarians (of whom I shall have more to say later), all of us now gratefully acknowledge how much enrichment and deepened devotion they brought into the life of our fellowship. That, thank God, is no longer a party question. But what I wish to stress now is the way in which the Oxford centenary was observed. There had been fears, suspicions and misgivings, lest it should be made a sectional demonstration and thus an occasion of bitterness and division. It was, in fact, nothing of the kind. It became a festival of the Church of England, in which Churchmen of all " schools " and traditions thankfully and trustfully collaborated.

May we not claim this as significant of the new spirit and temper which have come to us? The partisan mind is a back number. Questions which but a short time ago would have been hotly and bitterly controversial are now discussed at every Church gathering sensibly, objectively and tolerantly, and with no desire to make party capital. It is not a question of a working compromise between incompatible schools of thought. It is that the many and diverse elements embraced in the Anglican tradition have come to see that each needs the others to complement its own contribution. The most trusted and influential leaders are today the men with synoptic minds—not partisans of dead controversies. The old outlooks may persist in backwaters, but not in the main stream of the Church's life. Quietly, unnoticed and unadvertised—the most fruitful growth being the least selfconscious—this new temper is gaining strength.

As it is still popularly supposed that the Church of England is the battleground of disputatious ecclesiastics—for Churchmen are " news " only when they quarrel or figure in criminal proceedings—it seems important to emphasise this. It is one of the factors that will count most in the religious life of the next decade. For what it means is that the Anglican Communion is becoming aware of itself, as no mere accident of history, no mere resultant of conflicting forces, but as the native Christian tradition of the Anglo-Saxon and English-speaking peoples with its own characteristic ethos and its own authentic contribution. All over the world it has taken root and has reproduced itself true to type. Even where it is not the Church of England but the Church of Canada or Australia, or the Protestant Episcopal Church of America, even when it contains other races and languages, as in India, China, Africa and Japan, it is still recognisably the same Church. It is thorough-bred and it breeds true. With whatever local varieties and differences—such as it is its genius to encourage —it persists, in its own specific identity and the funda-mental unity of its witness, liberal, catholic and evangelical.

(c) *Enrichment of Thought*. On the base of the font in Coventry Cathedral there are figures symbolic of the deadly sins, each bearing an appropriate emblem. Some of these were defaced or missing, and Victorian zeal has replaced one of them by a figure representing Heresy, who is shown reading from an open book, on

which is inscribed *Essays and Reviews*. We have
travelled quite a long way since then ! Not very many
contemporary Churchmen have so much as heard of
that publication which at the time caused such an
uproar. The bitterness of those days of controversy
and even the questions about which it raged are
almost beyond the comprehension of Christian
teachers and students in our own time. To us it
sounds wholly incredible that Bishop Wilberforce
wrote a savage attack on a book which admittedly he
had never read ! [1] Still more unbelievable is the
blindness of those who attacked this unhappy volume
to the new light that was breaking all round them.
" Their blindly conservative attitude," says Archdeacon Storr, " shows how English theology had for
years been standing aloof from all the larger
movements of thought in the world outside." Orthodoxy still took its stand on the literal inerrancy of
Scripture and that (apparently) in the Received
Text ; and it had no real appreciation of the pressure of thought on its closed system. What withstood
Darwin's hypothesis [2] was not Christian theology at
all, but an untenable theory about the Bible, and an
orthodoxy which all modern students would regard as
indefensible obscurantism. Yet it is all very recent
history ! The startling fact is that the journey from
Essays and Reviews in 1860, by way of *Lux Mundi* and
Foundations, to the recent *Essays Catholic and Critical*,

[1] *Cf.* Storr : *Development of English Theology in the Nineteenth
Century*, pp. 449-450.
[2] *The Origin of Species* was published the year before *Essays and
Reviews*. Newman's *Essay on Development* thus preceded it by
fourteen years.

was covered in not more than one normal lifetime.
Jowett's pupils are teaching in Oxford ; plenty of
men still in active work grew up under the influence
of Liddon—who was killed by the shock of *Lux
Mundi ;* and the outstanding figures of that group
have died only during the last year or two. (It
is hard for men of my own age to realise that
Bishop E. S. Talbot had been the first Warden of
Keble.)

We cannot attempt here even to summarise the
development of the last fifty years or the stages by
which there has been built up the constructive philosophical theology characteristic of the twentieth
century.[1] To it, all branches of learning have contributed. Biblical and historical scholarship—notably
that of the great Cambridge School, and of men such
as Charles, Driver, Peake and Sanday—re-laid the
critical foundations. Philosophy has rebuilt upon them,
turning away from the barren denials and insecure
reiterations which had brought theology into contempt to a frank acceptance of all truth from whatever
source it may be vouchsafed, strong in the faith that
the light that shines in Christ is indeed the true light
that lighteth every man. " I have always been (said
Gore) a free-thinker." Thus step by step there has
grown up a free, convincing, creative theology which
would be a glory to any Christian century. It may
be claimed without exaggeration that today English-
speaking Christianity can meet the best thought of
the twentieth century on its chosen fields—and out-

[1] See Carpenter, *op. cit.*, Chs. XVI and XVII, and C. J.
Webb, *A Century of Anglican Theology.*

think it. Indeed Philosophy and the Natural Sciences will soon have to confess before all the world that without the contribution of Christian thought none of their own constructions can stand. The initiative has passed to Theology. Not since the mighty achievement of St. Thomas has theology been so vital or so catholic.

It seems to be true that each generation thinks of itself as a race of Epigoni, and this induces a salutary humility. We deplore a lack of " great " men today, and there seem to be few among us of the stature of a Gore, a Creighton or a Westcott. Yet it may be that fewer great minds stand out towering over their contemporaries because the average level is so much higher. And in fact it would be exceedingly difficult to name any Christian generation which could point to a greater number of teachers of the first rank in all branches of Christian learning than the English-speaking Churches possess today. If one attempts to compile a summary list of men actively teaching at this moment who might be cited in evidence of this claim, the result becomes positively spectacular.

Our own Communion is nobly represented, and may claim to be coming into its birthright as essentially the Church of the new learning. But in this task all Churches have cooperated, discovering in it a new sense of fellowship which is bringing an unlooked-for reward.

(d) *Movements towards Reunion.* This enrichment and widening of range in the intellectual life of the Churches has brought to them all an enlarged vision of the Christian Society itself. What has been most hopeful and significant during the last quarter of our century has been the growing strength of the reunion movement. To this many factors have contributed. It is partly due to the liberation inspired by better-trained historical scholarship and a more sensitive intellectual conscience. We are coming, at long last, to recognise that there cannot be different kinds of truth, each the prerogative of one Church—as though there could be a Presbyterian truth, an Anglican, a Baptist or a Lutheran. There is truth, and all Christian thinkers are colleagues and partners in its service. As all have been learning from one another, each contributing the distinctive gifts of his own tradition and inheritance, they have been released from the controversial spirit. Few theologians are now concerned to uphold sectional interpretations of a truth which is greater than all our apprehensions of it. This theological cooperation transcending old denominational frontiers has engendered a new temper of trust amongst the leading minds in all Churches. The scholars have been proved to be men of action.

Pragmatic motives have also been at work. The Churches have all learnt from the discipline of straitened resources in both money and men, which has opened their minds to the wastage and futility in our duplicated organisations and our overlapping and even competing ministries. The Churches have found that they are too weak to face the stupendous task that confronts them and the mighty forces arrayed in opposition with their scattered and disunited armies. They have learnt the need for

" unity of command." Where the Church has been most " up against it," the drive towards unity has become most urgent. Most potent of all has been the recognition that, in a world torn by fear and hatred, the Church as the reconciling society is not only frustrating its own mission, but bringing reproach on the name of Christ by its divisions and its broken fellowship. The conviction grows that our divided Christendom is not merely a practical inconvenience, but a reproach, a shame and a scandal, a betrayal before the world of our profession. Thus the Great Church is beginning to awake, and Christians in all denominations are learning to offer constructive loyalty to that one holy catholic Church in which for so long we have professed belief.

The movement is going forward throughout Christendom, even within the Roman Communion, despite its official and public intransigence. If it is still at the stage of " pacts " and has not yet reached the " Geneva " method, it is not therefore necessarily the weaker, and may even be stronger and more realistic. The more the interconfessional differences between local Churches are resolved, the fewer become the occasions of friction, and the greater the hope of coalescence into an ecumenical reunion. In our own Church, as we have already observed, there has been during the last 25 years a notable re-centring of outlook and achievement of a common mind. This has been matched by a coming together within various separated Churches. The formation of the United Church of Canada, the Methodist reunion in England and the Presbyterian in Scotland, are perhaps the most signal examples. The areas of division are already narrowed. Negotiations have long been in progress between our Church and the English Free Churches, and were initiated (even if no more) between the two territorial Churches north and south of the river Tweed. Even though the official " conversations " with their almost inevitable set-backs appear to be tedious and disappointing, yet in various unofficial ways, and through agencies such as the " Friends of Reunion," much is being achieved under the surface, and a practical friendship and cooperation such as would in the past have been inconceivable are almost universally taken for granted. No doubt it is true that the rank and file in the Churches concerned are as yet but half-awakened ; but a new resolve has been born which must prove to be irresistible in the long run. Meanwhile, close and intimate understanding is established between the Church of England and the Episcopal Scandinavian Churches ; communion is already in sight between the Orthodox and the See of Canterbury ; and, what is perhaps most significant, it has now been formally restored between ourselves and the Old Catholics.

In the mission-field, where the old differences are at once most crippling and most irrelevant, the will to unity is most masterful. The most conspicuous and impressive evidence is the scheme, now approaching realisation, of the United Church in South India. But everywhere it is being recognised that the work of any one Church is but part of a worldwide Christian movement, and can be fruitful only within that context.

All that is vital in the Christian mission is interconfessional and inter-national.

Here the Churches owe an immense debt (which they have not too generously repaid) to the World Student Christian Federation, with its vision of students gathered from all lands in a great interdenominational fellowship as Christian leaders and servants of their own people. It has been the pioneer in this kind. Many of those who are doing big things for the Kingdom of Christ among the nations, many of those who are giving effective leadership to the cause of Christian reunion, have been trained by the British Student Christian Movement of the World Student Christian Federation. The latter was almost the only religious organisation which preserved its international contacts during the fury of the world war ; and it did a work of outstanding value in reconstruction and reconciliation in the wild, embittered years that succeeded it. It has stood for an international Christianity when even the Churches had become nationalist. That conviction is now part of a common legacy. The ecumenical movements and conferences known as " Lausanne," " Stockholm " and " Jerusalem " are at once symbols and instruments of the vision, gaining in strength and clarity, of a reborn fellowship in Christ—that one true Church universal in which all our paths must converge, and the nations shall bring their glory and honour into it.

Thus, in whatever direction we look, the Christian record during the past century is one both of expansion and consolidation. The year 1935 finds the

Church of Christ in the world—and not least the Anglican portion of it—alive, hopeful, forward-looking, flexible as an instrument of God's will in the distracted and bewildering world which it is now being summoned to redeem.

2. CHRISTIANITY AND THE NEW AGE

The century that has elapsed since the accession of Queen Victoria has seen the most cataclysmic changes of any period in the human record. Mankind has passed within living memory through such a revolution in outlook, such an upheaval in all the conditions of life, as would hitherto have needed a thousand years. From the stone age to the death of Queen Victoria (as Gerald Heard observes) is one era ; we are now living in the second.[1] The advanced thought of twenty-five years ago is the obscurantism of today. The emotional patterns of the earlier period no longer fit the conditions of our experience. The established forms of social behaviour seem unadapted to the new *tempo*. The moral axioms of our grandparents no longer present themselves as axiomatic. It had hitherto been assumed that each generation would live its life substantially under the same conditions as those which it had inherited from its predecessors and would pass these on to its successors. We are living (says Prof. Whitehead) in the first period of human history for which these assumptions are false.[2] Violent and terrific new forces are hammering out

[1] *These Hurrying Years*, p. 1.
[2] *Adventures in Ideas*, p. 117.

the moulds of a new world-order, and we cannot foresee what will be the form of it. Will it be an impersonal and soulless mechanism in which personal values are discounted and liberty is but a dead dogma? Will it break down in anarchy and bloodshed? Or will Spirit regain the mastery and shape process to its own purpose? That is the crucial problem of the new age; and the answer rests with the forces of religion.

We are groping after a spiritual ideal and a principle of social organisation with which to fashion that new form of Community which is now beginning, with so much confusion and so much suffering and ill-adjustment, to emerge on to the stage of history. Admittedly we are not yet succeeding. What has come to be called the new morality is at present crude, negative and defiant. The relation between the political state and the communities on which it is based, whether cultural or economic, is still a matter of hopeless uncertainty. We have not yet learnt to relate nationality to the world-community, recognised as inevitable, but prevented as yet from becoming actual at once by crude, atavistic passions and by that imperfect organisation which does so much to enhance their ferocity. The task seems too great, both for our intelligence and for our moral and spiritual resources. For what is decisive now is human quality. The more complicated life becomes, the more searching is the demand that it makes on character. And amid the onrush of our new knowledge the most startling discovery is this—that the outward framework of circumstance which has served both to protect us and to limit us, is itself transient and fluid. The supposedly solid, external world of Nature proves to be the construction of our minds. Political, social and economic conditions are born out of our own half-conscious impulses. Circumstances are ourselves in action. As never before in the history of our race we know now that Character is Destiny. At every point we are thrown back on ourselves.

Before that terrifying recognition it is not surprising if man's spirit weakens. " Before the magnitude of the tasks ahead man's spirit has for the moment faltered and his vision contracted. The public mood is apprehensive where it should be bold, and defensive where broad and generous policy is most required." [1] If all depends on the man within, and if within ourselves we are still aware of the wolf, the ape, the tiger and the donkey, then our prospect is indeed lugubrious. We have had to learn through fear and suffering that we cannot be our own redeemers. Frustrated and indecisive, we are unable to break our way out through the walls of inertia and despair. Such a renewal as the world waits for cannot be generated from within : it must be appropriated from without. Mankind needs more than anything else such a revival of faith in God, creative, victorious and transforming, as shall lift it out of despondency and helplessness and set it bravely to work upon the world again. It is the decisive hour for Christianity. Everywhere in the world it has reached the point when it must go forward to win or perish. And indeed the supreme

[1] Salter : *Recovery*, Epilogue.

issue of the new age is the victory or defeat of Christianity. On this more than on anything else whatever hangs the future of human civilisation. The Church cannot stand on the defensive. If in these ambiguous nineteen-thirties anything can be confidently predicted, it is that any faith or institution content to stand merely on the defensive is doomed, irrevocably and beyond hope.

this is true today. (1971)

But there is no need for such craven tactics. The initiative is with the Christian forces. All other solutions are bankrupt and all other prescriptions discredited. Every day demonstrates more clearly the emptiness and sterility of life devoid of ultimate spiritual conviction. In the midst of all our exuberant interests the heart of the world is numbed and disillusioned. What Gregory of Tours said about the decline of the Imperial system might be quoted truly about our age : *In cordibus aruerat*—it had gone dead in the hearts of men.[1] With the decay of faith in a living God and a sovereign purpose for mankind the world of today is all at cross-purposes, its thought confused, its values blurred, its aims wavering and indecisive. Yet it is everywhere being realised that only by the recovery of conviction and the release of spiritual forces can the twentieth century be saved. Thoughtful people are everywhere conscious that our grotesque economic chaos—in which millions are condemned to penury because (we are told) there is too much to eat—is a symptom of something far more fundamental—a profound moral and spiritual malaise. The intensified international antagonisms which

[1] Quoted by Christopher Dawson : *Enquiries*, p. 209.

threaten to bring civilisation down cannot be resolved except by conversion and rebirth into a new attitude. Security is essentially a moral problem. In every nation the great majority care for peace more than for anything else : yet we are moving headlong to war. In face of both these stupendous dangers the political expedients are bankrupt. The tasks that await mankind are insoluble by contradictory technical pronouncements and the faithless chicanery of politics. They can be achieved only on the plane of sheer moral and spiritual conviction : " So is the will of God and so it must be ; it is right, it is possible and it shall be done." There is nothing but faith in a living God which can offer the moral and spiritual dynamic to lead mankind out into the new age.

The peoples are waiting for a deliverer. Unemployment, penury and frustration are slowly sapping hope and vitality, while the ambiguous dogmas of economists confuse their minds but offer them no deliverance. Haunted by the spectre of war, they are yet allowing themselves to be persuaded to adopt the methods most certain to produce it. Yet there is in the hearts of the common people a profound distrust and dissatisfaction, and a growing sense that leaders have failed them. They are waiting for convinced leadership, as Germany shows only too clearly. If a voice were found to speak with authority across the confused and vacillating utterances of experts, theorists and politicians, to bring home to the heart and mind of the plain man the deep revolutionary simplicities of the things which belong to his peace, there would be such overwhelming response as has never been imagined in history. Christianity may yet be that voice. It may be the emancipator of mankind—" to give light to them that sit in darkness and to guide their feet into the way of peace." There is given to English-speaking Christianity an opportunity utterly unprecedented for creative spiritual leadership. It is ours, at least, to lead our own people and to bring them back to Christian conviction through vital reinterpretation of the legacy which we have inherited. And the English people are still far more Christian than they themselves or the Clergy admit.

3. DEFEAT OR REVIVAL ?

There is set before us an open door. Yet at first sight, it must be admitted, such a phrase seems the exact reverse of the truth. We can hear the doors banging all round us. Amid the play of reactionary forces which seem to be closing in on the world the weak, scattered influences of religion might appear almost futile in powerlessness. It has been sardonically observed that my book *The Relevance of Christianity* was published just at the precise moment when it became conspicuously irrelevant. Over a great part of the world today the idea of free spiritual community is not merely discredited, but scorned. The dominant thought of the moment is collectivist. Both in religion and in secular politics liberalism is damned as well as dead. The young, who but a few years ago seemed to be so impatient of authority as to imperil the whole social structure, now passionately

disbelieve in freedom.[1] What fills the whole contemporary horizon is the rise of the totalitarian state,
whether in its Communist or Fascist form—for both
of them rest on the same philosophy—persecuting rival
religions because it is itself a religion. Hobbes and
Machiavelli have returned, and the Church now finds
itself confronted with a modern form of the worship
of the Great Beast. *The Great Leviathan* is a far worse
menace to the whole Christian conception of life than
were ever the claims of romantic *Eros*. In many
parts of the world the stage is set for the old conflict
between Christ and Cæsar ; and it looks as though the
Church would be vindicated not so much by the
vigour of its leadership as by the courage of its
martyrdom.

The outlook is sufficiently discouraging. Yet it is
the gateway of opportunity. For the real underlying
cause of that reactionary temper which seems to be
paralysing mankind is the bankruptcy of non-theistic
Humanism. The world is sick with the fever of disillusionment. We have tried to believe in Man instead
of God and are now unable to believe in either. Broad
humanitarian ideals seemed to offer the last generation
a substitute for the supernatural faith which it could
no longer accept. But humanitarian ideals are not
winning in the world today. At point after point
they are being defeated. It is hard now to believe

[1] " Fascist and Communist, the young, illiberal regenerated
world split into these two camps, mutually fearing and loathing
one another but reserving their contempt for such as her, for the
drifting individualists who uttered the foolish cry of ' liberty.' "
Rose Macaulay : *Going Abroad*, p. 306 (of Mrs. Buckley and her
son Giles).

in human nature. The "strong" state rests on a fundamental scepticism of the capacity of human nature,
whether morally or intellectually, to sustain the
responsibility of self-government. With the decay of
ultimate conviction life was becoming a meaningless
process in which the individual man or woman had
ceased to count and had no part to play. Hence the
appeal of Fascism and Communism, which seemed to
implant some mystic touch at the heart of politics
and economics. " Deprived of the moral inspiration
of the old religion, yet dissatisfied with the alternative
of a self-centred individualism, these (countries) have
long been seeking for a dynamic ideal to save them
from personal and national demoralisation. Fascism
and Communism have power because they present
such an ideal and present it practically *as a religion.*"[1]
Young Communists and young Nazis describe the
rebirth which they have experienced in the classical
language of religious conversion. But the State on
whose altar they are dedicated is but " a swollen and
distorted form of one function of Society."[2] The
absolute State denies human nature : as it claims to
rule men's souls and consciences it usurps, whether
implicitly or explicitly, the sovereign claims of
spiritual reality, and thus involves such repudiation
of all that constitutes true humanity as to make
personal values chimerical. But, apart from belief
in God and immortality, all talk of freedom becomes

[1] Streeter, in *Personal Ethics*, p. 12.
[2] From a paper by Revd. W. G. Peck in *The Student Movement*,
January, 1934, on " Patriotism and the Church," to which these
paragraphs are considerably indebted.

unmeaning. Unless there is a spiritual destiny beyond time for individual persons, the defence of the value of the individual becomes almost impossible to maintain. Without faith in God there is no bar to the omnicompetent claims of State-necessity.

Thus the recrudescence of Nationalism—threatening not only the peace of the world, but all that Christian civilisation stands for—is at bottom a question of religion. It denies mankind because it denies God. The absolute claim of the national sovereign State makes a common humanity impossible. But it rests on a fundamental atheism—the denial of a common world-purpose in which all nations are to be partakers. Nationalism, says Aldous Huxley, is the positivistic creed of the " new stupid "—a substitute for traditional religion but " even more obviously false and mischievous." [1] Apart from the Christian belief in God, Sovereign and Father of all mankind, there *is* no higher moral authority than the interest of the national group. To admit that claim is essential blasphemy. But only a true religion can transcend it.

And unless Nationalism *is* transcended Spengler's vaticinations will be verified ; our civilisation will very soon be done. For one thing, we shall have starved ourselves to death, and the four horsemen of the Apocalypse will soon be riding across a stricken world. Here we encounter the insane paradox that, the more the world understands its economic interdependence, the more madly it attempts to violate the elementary principle of recovery. There can hardly be one educated person in any country in the

[1] *Beyond the Mexique Bay*, p. 107.

world today who believes that economic nationalism is anything but a policy of suicide. Yet all nations assiduously pursue it. Our proved dependence on one another, the means of transport and communication, the Cartel, the machinery of exchange and all the subtly interlocking forces which have made the world one economic organisation, have not yet made it a community. For what the nations have chiefly in common is precisely that which serves to divide them. Their common economic necessity is what sets them at one another's throats. Maddened by fear, they exhaust their vitality in straining after a self-contained economy which is, in the very nature of things, impossible, attempting to make economic frontiers march with those of political organisation. But there are no economic frontiers ; and were it not for the terror of war—itself the result of economic terror— no sane Government would try to defend them.

As it is, behind artificial barriers of tariffs, quotas, subsidies and restrictions, Governments are saving their faces while the populations are being sapped by privation, insecurity and panic. That is the way towards dissolution. The demoralisation of Central Europe is born of fear driven mad by hunger. Nor is it confined to Central Europe. Other countries, too, have their Dillingers : other nations have seen barricades : we do not know how far the disease will spread.[1] Civilisation, as Christopher Dawson says,

[1] " When people are brought up on creeds which they cannot believe, they are left with no creeds at all, and are apt to buy pistols and take to banditry, bag-snatching and racketeering when employment fails and they find themselves short of money." G. B. Shaw : *On the Rocks*, Preface, p. 168.

is facing the worst dangers that have threatened it—
war, revolution and starvation—with no inward
resources at its command and with no higher appeal
than self-interest.

Yet beside this judgment we may set another. The
decisive factor in the situation is not so much the
public anxiety as the amazing volume of goodwill,
courage, patience, cheerfulness and loyalty amongst
private citizens of all nations, which awaits only the
touch of conviction to be summoned into victorious
effectiveness. Here is the chance for spiritual leadership. " I believe (says Sir Arthur Salter) that in a
crisis which is psychological as well as economic the
real constructive forces in the world have been under-
estimated and only need to be evoked to make our
task possible." [1] What can evoke those still untapped
resources? It is the essential creed of Christianity
that the forces of life, renewal and construction are
stronger than those of reaction and decay. That is
the Gospel of the Resurrection. What the world is
waiting for is a rebirth of vital, convincing Christianity
to give men back a purpose to live for and the knowledge of a Power that can redeem us, to restore them
to faith, fellowship and freedom.

When the Christian says, " I believe in God," he
does not mean (as is frequently suggested) I am so
afraid of the facts of life that I want to fly to the arms
of a fantasy and take refuge in an imagined wish-
fulfilment. What he asserts is the exact opposite.
He means, " I believe that this is a real world and I
resolve to live a real life in it. I believe this world is

[1] *Recovery*, seventh edition, Preface.

coming out somewhere, as the sphere of a spiritual purpose, and that this purpose is made manifest in the life and spirit of Jesus Christ, in His death and in His resurrection. Therefore, I take my courage in both hands and commit myself to that cause. I believe that the lifegiving and redeeming forces which are at the heart of a spiritual universe are mightier than those which seem to resist them, and that men who are in touch with Christ are in touch with unconquerable resources. In that faith, therefore, mortal men may triumph and live victoriously and creatively."

CHAPTER II
THE CHURCH IN THE NEW AGE

1. CHURCHMANSHIP, TRUE AND FALSE

THE one really formidable argument against the truth of the Christian religion is the record of the Christian Church. Again and again it has denied its Lord, distorted His teaching and betrayed His Spirit. Again and again it has taken the wrong side. The Church as an organised institution has too often appeared not merely irrelevant, but positively injurious and obstructive to the cause of Christ in the world. History reveals with sombre monotony how easily the thought of ecclesiastics drifts out of line with the mind of Christ. Men may be forgiven for thinking that it is inherent in " organised religion " to pervert the original spirit of the Founders. Moreover, it has unfortunately been true that much of the teaching about the Church given by its official representatives has shocked the Christian conscience of the plain man. It has sometimes treated secondary questions as though they were fundamental Christian issues—straining a gnat and swallowing a camel. It has sometimes forgotten the Gospel altogether. There is a deep suspicion in many minds that assertions made on behalf of the Church have often little to do with Christianity and may even seriously misrepresent it.

What is known as " definite Church teaching " has
produced a great many very indefinite churchmen.
In the minds of too many modern men and women
the ecclesiastical forms of Christianity have come to
be most disastrously associated both with triviality of
concern and with questionable sincerity in expression.
Further, the notorious inability of the Christian
Churches to realise in act, either in social or economic
relations, the brotherhood which their pulpits proclaim, brings the whole idea into derision.   Many
sincere disciples of Christ think it better that they
should remain outside, where they feel less compromised and more honest.   The idea of the Church
has somehow gone wrong ; the whole conception is
under a cloud at present ; and for one or another of
many reasons the claim of institutional Christianity is
exposed to widespread distrust.   Not only among half-
educated critics who have never taken the trouble to
understand it, but among some of the finest Christian
spirits.   Indeed, one of the chief facts to be reckoned
with in the existing religious situation is that to many
faithful disciples the word Church and the word
Christianity seem to stand for two different things.
A very dangerous fissure is here opening between the
clergy and the lay people.

No one who cares for the future of religion can
acquiesce in this situation.   The Churches as we know
them in Britain are predominantly middle-aged
societies, and much that is most hopeful and promising
in contemporary life and religion stands in no conscious relation to them.   Unless the process can be
redirected, the Churches will soon cease to count at

all. They must face a steadily declining membership
in which the death-rate far exceeds the birth-rate ;
and while they last they must be the refuge of the
least adventurous elements in religion. Nobody who
is committed to Christ's cause and the Christianisation of the social order can regard this prospect
without profound misgiving.

But if we would reconstruct the Church idea in the
loyalties of the rising generation, no mere traditionalism will serve us. For them the appeal to history
does not hold. It may be true, historically speaking,
that the whole solid strength of Christianity has been
embodied in the Christian Church. But that, they
reply, is no argument : whatever it may have been in
the past, it has now outgrown its usefulness. The
appeal to support an ancient institution, whether it
be political or religious, on the ground that it cannot
otherwise survive, will be met by raising the previous
question : Has the institution any survival value ?
Social and political institutions and the moral ideals
with which they are bound up find themselves here
in the same case as the Church. All established
traditions are suspect, and those that seem to the
young to be most compromised by the moral *débâcle*
of 1914 are most likely to fall into condemnation.
No claim presented in such terms is compelling.
Along such lines we shall find the road blocked.
Moreover, what tells heavily against us is the deep
suspicion of propaganda. The result of experience in
the war has been to make it almost an axiom in the
minds of thoughtful and educated people that official
propaganda *must* be untrue. It is probable that this

counts for more than the clergy have as yet realised
in contemporary reaction against the Church. Many
undergraduates think of the Church as merely part
of a general conspiracy organised by the War Office.
Thus there seems to be very little hope if we argue in
terms of an institution which is just "there" and asking
for our submission. We must get back behind thread-
bare arguments and candidly face the fundamental
questions : What is the place of the Church in the
modern world? and Does Christianity need a Church
at all?

Let us be clear what is at stake in all this. It is
not merely a clerical anxiety. It is not that we wish
the new generation to accept with more docility and
receptiveness the traditional teaching of the clergy,
which is not in itself necessarily a true aim. For, as
Cromwell told the Scots ministers, it is possible we
may be mistaken. The issue here is far more momen-
tous. We are concerned with something no less than
the reconstruction of our social order on its true
spiritual basis, and the Christianisation of the world's
life. When we look at the chaos of the world today,
is it not clear that its deepest need is for a society to
revive within it which rules its life by spiritual convictions? The root cause of our present confusion is
that politics, economics and ethics are in no true
relation to one another and are all unrelated to
religion. Our civilisation has no centre. The modern
way of escape from this confusion is by way of
recourse to the omnicompetent State, which can apply
the methods of compulsion over the whole field of
communal life because modern men are only agreed

on those material and economic interests to which compulsory methods are applicable.[1]

When people believe that the chief end of man is to glorify God and enjoy Him forever, then there can be spiritual unity, with large freedom for persons and groups within it. When they believe, as John Locke asserted, that the end for which men unite in commonwealths is the preservation of their property, then the State must become God.[2] The new civilisation which is emerging cannot find both unity and freedom till it is centred upon the will of God. Its fundamental need is redemption from destructive and sterile self-sufficiency, with the consequent international antagonisms, into the freedoms of the Kingdom of God. But in our age of high-power mass-production no merely individual insights can withstand the pressure of collectivism. At a time when all alert political thinking is intensely preoccupied with the Group (whether economic or national), it is strange that so many in their religious thinking are swinging out towards an individualism which in other spheres of life they reject. It is partly, no doubt, a desire to keep a way open by which they can escape from the pressure of mechanisation and regimentation and (as we say) " live their own lives " in the things of most intimate concern to them. It is, nevertheless, a mistaken attempt. For it is the task of the Christian society to provide for its members a common life which offers a richness of self-fulfilment greater than

[1] A. D. Lindsay : *The Churches and Democracy*, pp. 53 *sq.*
[2] I owe the juxtaposition to Mr. Buchan's *Oliver Cromwell*, p. 22.

anything which can be made accessible in a State-enforced uniformity.

In face of the mighty drive towards Fascism, individual religion is helpless.[1] Christianity can barely survive amid the intolerant blizzards of mass rule, such as threatens its existence in Europe and may yet sweep across our own land, save as a society conscious of itself and organised by its own transcendent allegiance. Nothing but a revival of the Church can withstand the usurpations of Cæsarism. What is needed to redeem and mitigate the overriding claims of the State are vital, free associations within the community which the State rules, acknowledging loyalties so strong that they will not burn incense to Cæsar. This, as the Master of Balliol has pointed out in the lecture from which I have already quoted, is the one hope of salvation for democracy ; and the genius of the Christian society is democratic, not authoritarian.

There is this further and all-important point. The Church as the one international society is the one force which can resist effectively the dangerous pretensions of nationalism. It has been the Anglican achievement to combine tradition and experiment, freedom and order, in vital synthesis. And the world-

---

[1] *Cf.* John Strachey's remark, " Life, with the growth of large scale production, is becoming less and less individual and more and more communal again. Thus for anyone who can achieve religious belief at all the Catholic form of Christianity is becoming increasingly appropriate." *The Coming Struggle for Power*, p. 161. But I am not arguing for a highly organised monarchical Church *vis-à-vis* the modern corporate state, but, as the text should make clear, the opposite.

wide Anglican Communion, conscious of itself as a
world-wide Church, yet united only by spiritual bonds
of faith, loyalty and a common order, is endowed with
unique opportunities as the nucleus of a universal
society transcending political and racial differences.
This is what the Church is intended to be. It is, in
ideal, the world-community with its life centred in the
divine Reality, thus at once transcending and redeeming all positive, secular societies, though it must
embody itself in them. And it is, in fact, the unique
instrument through which societies can be redeemed,
as being itself the redeemed Society gathered out of
every people and tongue. It is the witness to God's
reign on earth and the foretaste of its realisation.

Here, however, we reach the bigger question : Is
the Church necessary to Christianity ?

There are a good many people today who might be
prepared to give weight to the suggestion that the
Church may have a pragmatic importance. What
they find it impossible to accept is that belief in the
Christian Church is integral to the Christian religion.
The grounds for this contemporary attitude are, as
we have seen, not hard to appreciate. Yet it stands
in startling divergence from the Christianity of the
New Testament. If a man is a Fascist or a Communist, then the Fascist or Communist state is central
in his political philosophy. He cannot accept Communist or Fascist principles and remain detached from
the organisation. So it is with the Church in the
New Testament. As it is called into being by the
Gospel, so it is part of the Gospel which it preaches
and an essential element in its own creed.

In religion, however, the man of the modern world wishes to try this strange experiment of believing the principles of Christianity and disbelieving in that society in which alone they can be incarnated. Many signs, in England at least, suggest that we are now standing on the threshold of a great revival of faith and conviction. The crushing sense of futility and failure which hangs like a fog over public affairs is forcing back the rising generation on a search for the ultimate springs of hope and freedom. People are hungry for a living religion, for a God to pray to and a faith to live by and a power to recreate the social order. Nobody who is in touch with the Universities can fail to observe how the young men and women are turning back to seek almost desperately for the secrets of Christian faith and life. And the tide is coming in very fast. But to watch it fills one both with hope and fear. The Christianity which they are rediscovering is in most ways magnificently vital. It is sincere, spontaneous and self-sacrificing. It is ready for big response to big claims. But it has, on the whole and summarily stated, very little regard for the Christian Church. To most of the younger people in our time the Christian religion presents itself in terms of an individual relationship between themselves and the Christ they seek to follow. For the Church, at least as traditionally conceived, they are unable to see the necessity. Admittedly it may be of some value that people who hold a conviction in common should associate for mutual encourage-ment and the wider propagation of their beliefs, as in a political party or a trade union. But the

Christian life can quite well dispense with this. Church membership seems to be regarded more or less as an optional " special subject," not part of the prescribed Christian course.

Now all this needs very tender handling. We must never forget that religion is now passing through a reconstruction and readjustment in comparison with which the Reformation in the sixteenth century was but a tiny bubble. A restatement of belief is in process much further reaching and more fundamental than the still mediævally-minded Reformers dreamed of. There is, even more urgently than there was then, a demand for simplicity and reality and a concentration on " things that matter." There is, in common with the reforming movements, a determination to press back to Christ, to the Gospel and to the " pure " word of God, as the ultimate court of appeal. And all great revivals have come from a rediscovery of the mind of Christ, to revitalise a dead tradition or to check and purge a false interpretation. But there is this tremendous difference, that the critical scholarship of the last century brings us more closely into touch with the historical Jesus Christ of Nazareth than was possible for our Christian predecessors at any time in the past thousand years. And Christianity, after all, is Christ.

If a non-ecclesiastical Christianity, much concerned with the Spirit and teaching of Jesus and very little with organised religion, holds the allegiance of the younger people, there is no cause there but for hope and thankfulness. It is probably the best thing that could happen as the first step in a real resurrection of the Christian

Church which is His Body. It is urgently important at all times that the Christian conscience should be sensitive to the comparative failure of the Church to express in action the Spirit of its Lord, and exercised to redress that discrepancy. The Spirit of Jesus (as that great missionary Temple Gairdner loved to reiterate) is the only asset of the Church. But without the Church Christ is unfulfilled. And as part of the new Reformation there must be a creative reconstruction of our thought and teaching about the Church itself. It is not more arguments about Churchmanship that will offer the right way of approach, but more understanding of God and Christ and the method of God's work in the life of man. We must start not from institutional theories, but from Christ Himself and the Gospel.

The Church is necessary to Christianity because through it Christ's work is done and the Gospel which He proclaimed is verified. Without it both would be frustrated and unrealised. Christ proclaimed the coming of God's kingdom and offered Himself that it might come true. Whatever precisely the Kingdom of God meant to Him it implies, at the very least, transformed relationships between men and God and men and one another, brought into being by the divine initiative. The Gospel is the good news about God because of what Christ has revealed and wrought, that he who has seen Him has seen the Father, and that it is God who is in Christ reconciling the world to Himself. A Church that has ceased to exhibit that Gospel has forfeited its claim to men's allegiance. But apart from the Church, what Gospel is there ?

If no redeemed society had been born, then the Cross of Christ was defeat. Reconciliation is an empty word till it is verified in a common experience. But men learnt to say " God is Love " through what they learnt in the new community.

Wherever this Gospel has been proclaimed men have been drawn by it into a fellowship wherein, by a common partaking in Christ's Spirit, they are reconciled to one another. It was so that the Christian movement started. The Church as the New Testament presents it to us is conceived not as a voluntary society which a man may or may not decide to join, but as God's act through Jesus Christ called into being by His redemptive purpose. This is, for the New Testament, the evidence that God is at work in the world through Him ; here the eternal purpose of redemption clothes itself in visible form on earth. In a world of alienation and antagonism where men felt that they were estranged from God, a new society woke into life by the touch of God through Christ in the Gospel. In it the barriers were down, and in mutual trust and forgiveness men learnt the meaning of the divine love. It was something unprecedented and unique ; no fortunate accident of history, but the work of God whose will for the world—to call men into fellowship with Himself through Christ and thereby with one another—was thus being revealed and fulfilled. It was the divine will coming true, on earth as it is in heaven. This is the heart of Christian experience ; it is what Christ means in the lives of men. It is the starting point of the Gospel as it is its verification and fruition, the outward manifestation and the instru-

ment of the grace and truth which it proclaims.
Thus the Church is part of its own Gospel as the
means whereby mankind can be " saved," reconciled
to God and one another through Christ's redeeming
and lifegiving Spirit.   It is the organ of Christ's
work in the world.

To profess belief in the Church, therefore, is to live
in the faith that Christ will win, that in Him mankind
will be redeemed out of fear, hatred and antagonism
into a true community of the Spirit in which God's
love and justice will reign and the mind of Christ be
the law of liberty.   And it is to pledge one's life to
that cause.   This is no abstruse doctrine of theology,
but the consecration of discipleship.   And it is what
is vital and permanent in the Catholic doctrine of the
Church.

But this is not in the least inconsistent with the
great Evangelical tradition.   Some Christians are
apt to be afraid of it.   Partly because—as we shall see
later—it has frequently been stated in the wrong way ;
partly because they think it belittles that personal
intercourse of the soul with God without which there
is no real religion.   Let us first remove this misunderstanding.

There is no vital, developed religion which is not
" personal " religion, and certainly there is no
Christianity.   Religious progress has come not least
through the emancipation of religion from a merely
communal or group conception of it to the recognition of individual souls as the subjects of religious
experience.   Such a movement is reflected in the
Old Testament ; and the faith of Christ, which sets

supreme value on persons made for communion with God, is unalterably a personal religion. Yet, because personality is social, an individualistic religion may prove to be the very reverse of " personal." Men become persons in relationship. And because of the social nature of personality *all* " Grace " comes to men through societies. It is one of the laws of human experience that all appreciation and all knowledge, all our values and all our moral insights, are mediated by social inheritance ; and this is as true in religion as elsewhere.

The pioneer in the arts and sciences owes his epoch-making discovery to the tradition which he supersedes. The moral and religious reformer is the child of the society which he criticises. Even the flash of mystical intuition, which seems the direct immediate confrontation of the soul " alone with the Alone," is in fact mediated and made possible by the seer's religious inheritance. Everywhere in life this law holds. But it holds in a special sense of Christianity. The claim to " owe nothing to the Church " is almost unbelievably superficial. To what do we owe so much as the knowledge of Christ's name ? There are, no doubt, lonely " conversions " which seem to be entirely unmediated by any Church or any personal agent : they come, as St. Paul said, " by revelation." But even these are in fact due to the inspiration of some Christian deed (the manner of Stephen's death, for example), the memory of a Christian upbringing, a phrase in the New Testament, and so forth ; and these are the focus or embodiment of the spiritual legacy of the Church.

" Back to Christ " is an inspiring cry : but in fact we can only find Him if we go where His people are. If it means Back to the Synoptic Gospels, at least half their meaning evaporates—some would say that they become meaningless—if we ignore that common experience which they assume and from which they come. They were born out of the worshipping community. And as with them, so with the Christian life. It lies at the heart of Christian experience that God's redeeming gift through Christ Jesus comes uniquely to men and women when they share in His faith and fellowship. That, in essence, is what the Church means. Nobody with the New Testament before him can doubt that it was, and is, from the matrix of this inward spiritual community that the new life flows upon the world, with its new values and insights and transfigured qualities of character, to redeem and to redirect it from within. The Christian redemption of the social order is offered the world through this redeemed society.

In saying this, we do not delude ourselves with futile dreams of a revived Theocracy. The Church will never again " rule " the world in the sense that " one set of men (the clergy) laid down rules for another set of men," which was the mistake of the mediæval system.[1] It may be regarded as a false ideal to conceive of the Church as itself a social order —a society standing over against others and embracing all human activities is a characteristic polity of its own. That does not affect the main argument. For our present purpose it is not even necessary to use institutional language at all. We may think in terms

[1] Lindsay : *Christianity and Economics*, p. 144.

of a company of friends, drawn together in worship and fellowship by their most distinctive and precious possession and the bond of their common discipleship.

Nevertheless, it still remains true that the Church is the instrument of God's work, reconciling the world to Himself. Through the outward movement upon the world of that communion in the Christ-Spirit which is His supremely redemptive gift, there may be fashioned a transformed social order in which the changing materials of the world's life—biological, economic and political, with all the technical factors involved in them—may be made the incarnation of that Spirit and the outward embodiment of His will for men. That is implied in the phrase, the Body of Christ. It would be the Kingdom of God in the world's life. In view of this we may even say truly that the Church must *dominate* human history. For God's work in man through Christ Jesus is His uniquely precious and determinative but ever-renewed act in the world's life. All that is good is of His creation, summoned into life by His touch. But " through the Incarnation and by His Holy Spirit in the Church God is ever moving forth to conserve and to perfect all that He has achieved, and still strives to achieve, in hearts wherein Christ is not yet enthroned." [1]

2. THE CHURCH AS GOD'S ACT

This idea is often misrepresented. Those who are most sensitively alive to this rich conception of the

[1] Lambeth *Encyclical*, 1930, p. 20.

Church as the unique (but not the sole) instrument of God's Kingdom in the life of the world are apt to spoil their case by expounding it in " high and dry " institutional doctrine. This is why people are sometimes repelled by it. The danger in the " Catholic " type of teaching is that the Church should be represented as an almost impersonal and mechanical *system* through which " means of Grace " are conveyed. But such thought moves on a sub-Christian level. You can have a perfectly logical exposition of the way in which " Grace " is given through the Church, its ministry and its sacraments, which has yet no moral or spiritual content, and appears to have no vital connexion with the mind of Christ revealed in the New Testament. But the " Grace " of a living God is not impersonal, and no *system* can be a " channel " for it. Such a view is profoundly un-catholic ; and the evangelical, reformed Churches grew up not least by way of protest against this debased mediævalism. It is not thus that Christ dwells with His own.

The formative idea of the Christian fellowship is in the phrase "Where two or three are gathered." The Grace of God comes to Christian people through the life and worship of the Church because, when Christians meet together in the faith and in the name of Christ, That comes alive in their hearts which is liberating, " sovereign and life-giving " (κύριον καὶ ζωποιοῦν). " Means of Grace " through sacraments and ministries are derivative from that experience and the life of the Christian community ; and no theory about them can be true which is more " mechanical " than that is.

Moreover, interpretations of this kind seem to lead, with fatal facility, into that perversion of the Church-idea which conceives of it as a *clerical* society. The Church is a " priestly " society—that is, in respect of its whole membership : but it is not a clerical society. Few things have done more harm than the confusion between " Clericalism " and " Churchmanship." The English layman has an instinctive dread that what he vaguely calls " high church " doctrine will hand over his conscience to the clergy and enable them to impose views upon him which he knows in his heart to be inconsistent with the spirit and teaching of Jesus Christ. And for this he has a good deal of justification.

To some minds there is a strong appeal in the thought of a great institutional system, logical, consistent and authoritative. It appears to be intellectually imposing and an antidote to slack, flabby thinking. It is plausible, but it is fallacious, and in the end it gravely misinterprets the genius of the Christian religion. It makes, no doubt, for practical efficiency ; it seems to supply a fine fighting faith. When the Church is hard-pressed, the natural tendency is the tightening up of institutional stresses, with strong appeals for discipline and authority. But there is too high a price to be paid for it. Institutional authoritarianism is not the genius of Christianity.

It is of the very utmost importance to keep our thought of the Church uncontaminated by the virus of the " ecclesiastical " mind. The obstinate religious individualism so characteristic of our native temper is at heart a protest against that. The Englishman has seen it in action, insisting, in the name of the Church, on theories which are blankly incompatible both with the Christian idea of God and the realities of the Christian life. It appears to him an unchristian frame of mind. He has seen pre-occupation with a system result in unchurching fellow Christians who have thought right to order their common life on a different principle of organisa-tion. That may be irrefutable in logic, but he knows that it is simply untrue.

Hence, as the Bishop of Gloucester observes, the word Church, which ought to inspire a great vision of fellowship in Christ, comes to stand for something sectarian and implies separation and exclusiveness. The theologian who expounds its doctrine seems to dwell on what will keep people out of it, instead of seeking how many he can include.[1] If that is what the Church-idea stands for it seems to the Englishman to be something different from what he has learnt of Christ in the Gospels. He is shocked, also, by the triviality into which too often, as he observes, the ecclesiastical outlook degenerates. The things that clergy are apt to think important are frequently, so he believes, negligible.

The idea of the Church for which we are here contending is at every point contradictory to the merely ecclesiastical point of view. But it is in fundamental accord with the true " catholic " tradi-tion. The ecclesiastical temper and outlook are a perversion of genuine " catholicism." Nobody can be too " high " a churchman. You cannot hold too

[1] *What it Means to be a Christian*, pp. 165-166.

high a view of the Church, because it is God's act through Christ Jesus : it is not of ourselves, it is the gift of God. But the " higher " the view we hold of the Church, the more we appreciate its unique mission in the redemption of the world's life, the less " ecclesiastical " should we be, and the less concerned with the trivial interests and tawdry bric-a-brac of ecclesiasticism. A man may be a perfectly good churchman without ever reading a Church newspaper.[1]

Such are on the whole its best members ; and it is not the least of our weaknesses that we associate the idea of Churchmanship with ways in which people spend their spare time rather than with doing their job in the world well. But the latter is integral to the Church's life, and far more important to the Kingdom of God than membership in " Churchy " societies.

It has been the great contribution of the Liberal school in the Church of England to keep alive an essential protest against excessive rigidity and formalism. By its scholarship and historical research it has undermined many of those assumptions on which rigid theories had been based. It has been the brave

---

[1] " I have so much insisted upon *the Church* in my recommendations that it may look inconsistent if I warn you against Church Societies, Church newspapers—the little Churchinesses which, I should think, must be fairly frequent in your Cathedral Town. . . . To love Holy Communion, yet tactfully, unironically to escape from all Eucharistic Guilds, etc., to care for God's work in the world especially in and through Christianity, and yet (again quite silently, with full contrary encouragement to others who are helped by such literature) never opening a Church paper or Magazine. . . . I only want to clear away every possible half-notion that in order to love God, Christ, Church dearly, it is necessary for everyone (hence also for you) to be *Churchy*." Von Hugel : *Letters*, p. 289.

champion of freedom. Against obscurantists on both wings it has stood for the claim of intellectual liberty. To it chiefly we owe the vindication of biblical and historical criticism and a scrupulous regard for the laws of evidence. Its courageous and unfettered thinking has led the Church through the readjustments and reconstructions of its theology, enabling it to retain the respect of educated men and women and to hold its place in the Universities. Without its critical and prophetic spirit the Church would have hardly survived the crisis and would almost certainly have succumbed before the onslaughts of modern knowledge. We can hardly exaggerate the debt which we owe to it. Its great names are deservedly held in honour in English-speaking Christendom and beyond it. The weakness of this school, on the other hand, has been its rather inadequate and sterile interpretation of the Church itself, as at best a useful religious organisation and at worst a "necessary evil."

This is odd, from those who have done so much for the rediscovery of the New Testament. For the Church is conceived in the New Testament as " coming down out of heaven from God." It is God's act through Jesus Christ. The " grace of the Lord Jesus " and the " love of God " were experienced by the first Christians within the " community of the Holy Spirit."[1] It was " God who called them into fellowship through His Son Jesus Christ our Lord." Fellowship and Communion are the same thing, as they are translations of the same word : it means not merely a " brotherly " expansiveness, but

[1] 2 Cor. xiii. 14.

E.

a common partaking in that reality which creates the distinctively Christian experience. It is " communion in the Holy Spirit "—a mutual sharing in the new life imparted to men by God through Jesus Christ. And it was the direct, immediate result of the Lord's life and death and resurrection. On no other terms is it intelligible. No account of the Church can be true which does not directly connect it with Him ; and no interpretation of Christ Himself can claim any historical justification which does not account for the rise of the Christian Society.

It was out of the heart of that Community that there were born all those new insights, those new resources of faith and character, that sense of emancipation into new worlds which the Christians described as rebirth in Christ. It was what God, the self-imparting Goodness, could now evoke out of human history because of His work in man through Christ Jesus. It was not something imposed upon the Gospel, robbing it of its vital spontaneity : it was its verification and fruition. It was Jesus, coming to His fulfilment. Indeed, we may say without exaggeration that it was through this experience in community that they came to understand His significance. The Christology of the early Church grew with the deepening and widening of its own life.

And at this point it is well to insist that the claim of the Christian Society to become the universal community is bound up with its God-given origin. It claims to be the society for all men precisely because it " comes down from above." This cuts across twentieth century prejudice, but is really confirmed by human experience. Humanistic moral and religious systems are incorrigibly sectarian and exclusive. The chief concern of self-centred societies is the safeguarding of their own frontiers. They may do this by highly trained butlers quick to detect those who do not belong, or by rules of professional etiquette, or by visas, passports and Ellis Island ; but they all want to keep other people out as the best way of securing their own unity. The chief concern of the Christian society, at least when it is true to its own character, is to be going out into the highways and gathering in " both bad and good." It is not a society of select persons, but the home and school both of saints and sinners. It can hope to be catholic and all-including, irrespective of race, endowment or education, because it is not an earth-born society, but God's gift to man through Christ Jesus.

Contemporary thought seems to imagine that Christianity could be universalised and Christ brought near to the common man if we would drop those transcendent attributes with which Christian faith has invested Him and present Him frankly as "just like one of ourselves." But this is the contradictory of the truth about it. The categories employed in the New Testament to interpret the significance of the Lord rise in height and daring concurrently with the discovery of what He could do and the range of His redemptive influence. Men learnt to acclaim Him as " Son of God " when they discovered His universality and that He could be the Saviour of all the world. The same is true of the Christian Society. It can gather all mankind into its fellowship and make them partakers in its life because it derives through Christ from the Father. The divine claim of the Christian Society is the secret of its human availability.

The modern mind is obsessed by the problem whether the Church was " founded " by Christ, and doubts whether it can honestly be argued that He thought in terms of an organised society to preserve His teaching, and carry on His work. Those who think that this is non-proven can appeal plausibly and perhaps convincingly to the evidence of the Synoptic Gospels. But it is not a legitimate deduction that the whole idea of a Church is therefore a perversion of His thought and an "institutionalising" of His Spirit. That would not follow from the evidence. It might be perfectly true to His Spirit even though He had never expressly purposed it. After all, the developed Christian Society, as exhibited in the *Acts* and *Epistles*, was there first, and produced the Gospels. The reason why the Gospels were written was that people who had " learned Christ " already, within the experience of the community, wanted a portrait of Jesus of Nazareth and some account of the origin of the Movement. The reason why *these* Gospels were accepted was that they rang true to that experience.

But the desire for a negative conclusion is partly at least the reaction of honest men against the rather desperate special pleading to which traditionalism has had recourse. The forlorn attempts to call in as evidence teaching of which there is no trace in the records (which yet " may " or " must " have been given by Him during the period after the Resurrection) in order to make a traditional view plausible, suggests a case too weak for rational argument. People who have been brought up on such subterfuges naturally "see red" and lay about them as soon as they learn the rudiments of criticism.

The first necessity, therefore, is complete candour. I do not think it is possible to maintain that Jesus of Nazareth "founded" the Church in the sense in which (for example) John Balliol and Dervorguilla founded their College. He did not say Let us found a society. He did not provide it with statutes. He did not prescribe its organisation. It may be, as many scholars believe, that the eschatological colouring of His thought and abrupt foreshortening of His perspectives made it impossible for Him to foresee the emergence of any kind of religious community. That opinion can cite a good deal of evidence, though it ignores a good deal on the other side. (It would, for example, be very strange if a mind so saturated as His in the teaching of Deutero-Isaiah had not thought in terms of a "remnant" and the ministry of a redeemed community. It would be strange that He spent so much time in selecting and training the twelve unless He had some intention of using them. Nor is it easy to see why St. Peter wanted to fill up the place of Judas unless they had been led to expect that the twelve had some special part to play in the restoration of Israel.[1])

Yet even if we accept the extreme statement of the eschatological interpretation it does not invalidate the contention that the Church is the creation of His

[1] *Cf.* Luke xxii. 28.

Spirit ; which is all that is really fundamental for us. The Church existed in germ and nucleus from the day when He gathered His first disciples round Him ; and its life has been continuous ever since. " No other source than Jesus Himself can be found for those things which are most decisively original and vital in Christianity." [1] It is the constant *historical* reference which has kept the Church vigorous and creative, and whenever this has failed it has withered. The rite which lies at the centre of its cultus links its life finally and inseparably with Him who was crucified under Pontius Pilate. [2] This in itself makes it impossible to think of the Church as other than continuous with the " little flock " of the days in Galilee. Through friendship they had learnt faith. Through life in community with Him they had learnt to worship God as Our Father—the Father of our Lord Jesus Christ. Through the power of the Resurrection His redeeming presence became yet more intimate, and the love wherewith the Father had loved Jesus came to " be in them " and He " in them." This is the organic relationship between the prophetic ministry in Galilee and the community of the Holy Spirit in which His redemptive work was verified.

Christianity has never affirmed that Jesus of Nazareth in the days of His flesh is God's final word in human

[1] Grensted : *The Person of Christ*, p. 36.

[2] The so-called mystery hypothesis about the origins of the Christian cult is really too absurd to be taken seriously, especially after N. P. Williams' critique in *Essays Catholic and Critical*, pp. 392 ff. See also W. R. Matthews : *Essays in Construction*, Chs. X and XI. " If there is any continuation of the religion of Jesus in the world, the Catholic Church with its supernatural claims has by far the best title."

history. His own teaching implicitly denies it. The
story in the Gospels is unintelligible unless He thought
of Himself as " more than a prophet "—as the Inaugu-
rator of the New Age and the Bearer of a redemptive
mission. The mysterious apocalyptic language expresses His claim upon the future [1] : and its meaning
is most perfectly interpreted in the most intimate
passages of the Fourth Gospel. " It is expedient for
you that I go away." That Gospel has given the deepest
expression to the inner secrets of personal discipleship,
yet it is the most " churchly " book in the New
Testament. Its Christ speaks out of the heart of the
Christian community. It translates the eschatological
language of the Synoptic records into new terms—the
Spirit who comes to lead men into all truth and to
build up a community in Love, bringing Christ
nearer to men's hearts than ever in the days of His
life on earth, as the Vine of which they were the
branches.

This common partaking in the Spirit expressed
itself by intrinsic necessity in a community of worship
and service. Life was now experienced from a new
centre. God's Kingdom was coming into the hearts
of men, and the " powers of the coming age " had
begun to transform this world of time. " In Christ "
all things were becoming new. There were deeper
backgrounds to personality ; there were wider horizons of thought and enterprise ; there were moral
and spiritual capacities to be elicited out of human
nature which neither religion nor morals had yet
dreamed of. People who had never before " counted "

[1] See *Relevance of Christianity*, pp. 91-99.

—*things that are not*, in St. Paul's blunt description—
now became vitally individual.   For this Church was
a community of persons—not a " totalitarian " experiment like Cæsarism, Fascism or Communism, which
sacrifice men to collective policy.   It was a home, in
which men and women could be themselves and could
be their best :   the Gospel spoke in the language of
home—" in our own tongue wherein we were born."
Life, within it, assumed a new sacredness, and enterprise found a new incentive.   Men bred in an
atmosphere of despair, paralysed by the atrophy of
conviction, lost to the secret of moral regeneration,
could now get bravely to work on the world again.
A new chapter in history had opened.

The various documents of the New Testament
contain, as it were, the introductory paragraphs in
that still uncompleted chapter.   They allow us to see
the new scale of values which the brethren begin to
acknowledge, the transfigured qualities of character
which begin to appear in average men and women,
the moral and intellectual vitality evoked from them
by the lifegiving Spirit, the creative and regenerative
resources which are in the possession of the redeemed.
The full meaning has yet to be discovered : the complete
content of the new order has yet to be disclosed in
human experience.   But this Community in the Holy
Spirit was rightly described as God's " new creation."
It was God, at work in men's hearts through Christ,
who had gathered them into this experience.   The
Community was the act and gift of God reconciling
the world unto Himself, and the instrument of that
reconciliation.   And it is an act constantly renewed.

It is now, as it was then, out of common worship and friendship " in Christ " that the great liberations are born and the characteristic Christian responses to the pressure of God upon the world evoked.

To insist upon this is of the first importance. For the gravest obstacle to Christian faith is the annihilating sense of contrast between the " Jerusalem that is above " and the " Jerusalem that now is." It is difficult, as Dr. Matthews says, to resist the feeling of anticlimax in looking at the Church as it now exists " compared with the creative act which gave it birth "[1] It is now in bondage with its children. " The Churches," as we know them in the modern world, are massively organised institutional systems, working through a complex machinery of financial and administrative routine. This is not least true of the Church of England, with its rigid framework of legal precedent and its immensely strong social tradition. No one can understand the Church of England, or hope to achieve any reforms within it, till he has schooled himself to appreciate the enormous pressure and thrust of the traditional and the almost unbreakable resistance of its legal and administrative steelwork. That is not necessarily all to the bad. It may even pertain to its characteristic ethos as a Church which has consecrated for a thousand years the public as well as the private life of the nation. Yet its elaborate, complicated mechanism does seem frigid, impersonal and remote compared with the intimacy and spontaneity of the *Koinonia* in the New Testament. The idea of the Church on which we have been

[1] *Op. cit.*, p. 234.

dwelling seems too ethereal to survive embodiment in diocesan boards and sub-committees.

There is, of course, no real inconsistency between spontaneous spiritual inwardness and organised practical efficiency : spirit must always fashion itself a body. But organisation *can* stifle spirit ; and the very strength of our system is a danger to it. The essential simplicities of the faith of Christ may be, and too easily are, obscured by the complexity of the external instrument. It sometimes seems as though the official voice of the Church of England had forgotten how to speak the language of Galilee. Though it now represents but a small minority, " the Church " is one of our " national institutions " ; it is a great traditional organisation for supporting religion and other good causes ; it is honoured as such by the Press at its best ; and probably to a number of its own members it does not represent very much more than that. They would feel disconcerted and self-conscious if they were told that its business in the world is to embody the Spirit of Jesus Christ. Many of them may feel pride and confidence in the continuity of the Church they know with the stream of Christian life from the first days. But it is probable that the great majority think of the Church described in the New Testament as but the half-formed tentative beginning of the organisation which has grown out of it.

It therefore becomes supremely important to insist that the scriptural experience of community in the Holy Spirit, as the matrix of new and enriched response to life, is not merely the historical origin, but the regulative idea of the Church, at all times and in all places.

And if the Church is to retain vitality it must be continuously breaking through the massive framework of the organisation. For the Church is God's act at each point of time : though it is continuous, yet it is never finished. It is, as St. Paul said, yet to be fulfilled ; it is not a tradition merely, but a growth, an adventure rather than an institution. It is in the world as the vital nucleus of community perfected in God. It perpetuates itself in its environment as the manifold elements of the world's life are redeemed from the dominion of worldliness and incorporated into the " Body " of Christ.

3. INTROVERSION AND ITS REMEDY

For the Church is in the world to redeem it. A Church true to its character and mission will be looking outwards upon the world, not inwards upon its own system. If its interest becomes fixated on exclusively institutional concerns the outward flow of its life will be inhibited and it will be threatened with auto-intoxication. Thus an excessive preoccupation with ecclesiastical or institutional questions seems to connote an inadequate understanding of what is really implied in Church membership. So von Hugel observed of Dr. Pusey that " He was incapable, or had made himself incapable, or deliberately acted as though he were incapable, of taking any interest in anything that was not directly, technically religious and not explicitly connected with religion." And this, he comments, was quite uncatholic—" quite unlike the great catholic saints, quite unlike the Jesus of the Synoptists."[1]

That was, indeed, the disastrous mistake to be laid at the door of the Oxford Tractarians, whom we were commemorating so recently.   I am not now thinking of those royal men such as Gore, Scott Holland and E. S. Talbot, who were born later out of this tradition—eminent among our saints and prophets and the masters of my own generation—but of the group who produced the Tracts.   Of the latter it is not unfair to say that they made the Church of England self-conscious.   Looking out on a demoralised society in which (as they believed, rightly or wrongly) the influence of Religion was fatally weakening, they set out to revive and secure the Church.   They were men of profound spiritual experience, and some of them of heroic moral stature, whose candle is never likely to be put out.   They belong to the classics of religion. No incumbent of St. Mary's at Oxford can escape from the haunting influence of Newman[2] : no one who believes in the Church of England can forget Keble's tenacious anglicanism.   They did revive in our own Church and beyond it a devotion, a richness and a spirituality for which we owe them perpetual gratitude.

Yet it remains that their whole trend of thought was essentially backward-looking and reactionary. They believed that the right way to revive the Church

[1] *Letters*, p. 254.
[2] Out of all the innumerable books about him that which comes nearest to understanding Newman is Mr. Geoffrey Faber's brilliant study, *Oxford Apostles*.

as a living society in its own right, not a mere religious department of the State, was to close the ecclesiastical frontiers. They resisted all liberal speculation. They refused to recognise changing circumstances. They joined battle on mistaken issues. In face of nearly all suggested reforms, the Tractarian leaders took the wrong side. With the great issues stirring in the world in the pregnant period of the Reform Bill they seem to have felt no religious concern. It is, surely, a singular coincidence that at the moment when Mr. Keble was preaching about National Apostasy, the House of Commons was passing into law its most conspicuously Christian measure.[1]

It was the misfortune of the Tractarians that their instinct was to look backwards—to define the nature of a living society in terms of what they supposed it to have been in the Patristic and Conciliar periods. Thus they drew the Church away from current affairs and out of touch with the movements of life ; and the things that seemed to them most important are not those that have counted for most in history. They did not look out with prophetic vision over the forces astir in the world and ask How can the Church redeem them, and purify and secure what is of worth in them ? They thought of the Church as a static institution built on the apostolic succession, and their emphasis lay on its own interior logic. And thus— whether by design or accident—they introduced into the Church of England, and indeed into English

[1] The Abolition Act was introduced on July 5, 1833, second reading July 22. Committee stage, July 25. Death of Wilberforce, July 29. Keble's sermon was July 14.

Christianity, an introversion and self-concern, a pre-occupation with its own security, from which it has not yet fully recovered. It has meant a remoteness from living issues and an ecclesiastical self-centredness which—despite their rich contribution—has proved itself a ruinous legacy. It is this which is still chiefly responsible for the alienation of the English people from the corporate life and devotion of the Church, and that breach between lay and clerical Christianity which so weakens contemporary religion.

But an introverted Church has no future. The task that is committed to it on earth is the redemption of the social order ; and in dedicating itself to this mission it will be redeemed from self-conscious anxiety about itself and its organisation. It is probable, I think, that in future the institutional factor in the Church's life will come to seem less and less important. It may even be that " the Churches " must die that the Church may live in a redeemed world-order. Such speculations may or may not prove to be true. But in any case it is surely most necessary to be clear in our minds that the institutional questions are secondary and derivative, not primary and funda-mental. Their importance is strictly instrumental to the nature and purpose of the Church itself.

That has not always been clearly recognised. Indeed, it might be rather more accurate to say that a frank acceptance of this standpoint involves something like a reversal of accepted and customary ways of thought. In the past, the question What is the Church ? has been answered in terms of institutional structure. The Church, people have said, is a Society which is

organised in such and such ways. Inevitably the
conclusion has followed that a body of Christians
organised in some other way is not a " Church " (or
a " true Church ") at all. Hence all the confusion
and broken fellowship and reciprocal excommunica-
tions and rival claims to be the only true Church which
have disgraced the history of Christendom. Hence,
too, the exaggerated importance attached to questions
of precedent and validity which has so much sapped
the vitality of the Churches.

The mistake in all this was not in the logic. Great
Christians like Bishop Gore have accepted with
unconcealed reluctance conclusions which seemed to
be logically inevitable, even although they do not
correspond with the realities of Christian experience.
There was nothing wrong with the arguments, but
they led to conclusions which do not square with the
facts. The mistake must have lain in false premisses.
They sought to define the nature of the Church in
terms of its institutional organisation. But it is
function that determines structure rather than structure that determines function. The true nature of
any living system consists not in its organisation alone,
but in the end towards which it is tending and the
purpose by which it is organised. The nature of a thing
is its meaning—or, in Aristotelian language, its *Telos*.

What constitutes an organic, living whole is the
unity of the purpose informing it ; and conscious
self-direction towards an end is the prerogative of
mind or spirit. True, that the mind transcends its
outward expression. The purpose has always a
richer content than is ever fully expressed in the

system, and the medium of its self-expression may partially thwart or frustrate that purpose. The whole is not *identical* with its meaning. On the other hand, in no true whole are form and content ever completely separable ; it may be the case that with a different structure it would itself be something quite different. It is thus rather superficial thinking which assumes that the Church—or indeed anything else—could be taken to pieces and remade without ceasing to be what it is. Yet this does not invalidate the contention that enquiry into the nature of a system must at least have more regard to its purpose than to the forms through which it has been externalised. Therefore a true philosophy of the Church will be teleological rather than archæological. It will not be exclusively concerned with history nor with the forms of the existing structure. Its question will be What is the Church for ? It will therefore no longer be condemned to attempting to solve the practical problems of the Church in twentieth century civilisation by archæology and appeal to precedent. It will recognise that the right methods, the right ministries and orders of worship, are those which best serve its true nature in the midst of contemporary conditions, as the mediator of the Spirit of Christ, the sacrament of God's reality and the instrument of divine redemption in the manifold forms of the world's life.

The question, therefore, is not Which is the true Church ? It is rather How can the Church come true ? Looking at the divided, fragmentary Churches into which the Christian fellowship has been broken, we shall not ask Which of all these Societies can claim to be the true Church of Christ? We shall ask by what means they can grow together into that which the Church is meant to be—the measure of the stature of the fullness of Christ.

The self-concern and the self-scrutiny with which the Church is at present afflicted are the symptoms of a morbid condition. Religion must be dangerously unhealthy when it keeps on asking how it can save itself. When it is vital, vigorous and virile the Christian Church will be least self-conscious, so absorbed in its saving mission that it finds its life in self-forgetfulness. It will not now regain its vitality by arranging conferences about itself, nor will it strengthen its authority by overmuch taking thought for the preservation of its own life. For the Church, as for its members, the law holds that they who are willing to lose their lives find them. Thus the way of renewal for the Church is by giving itself with imaginative courage to the leadership and redemption of the new age, with all the demands of adventurous faith implied in that tremendous vocation.

But this must mean for the Church a rediscovery of the Gospel which it exists to proclaim, and of the Purpose whose instrument it is; and, above all, a new liberation into the vision of the Glory of God.

F

CHAPTER III

THE MAJESTY OF GOD

1. THE NEED FOR THEOLOGY

CHRISTIANITY does not stand in the world for one more platitudinous reminder that it is better to be good than bad. It stands for a gospel about God. " This is life eternal, to know thee the only true God, and Jesus Christ, whom thou hast sent." That is the voice of authentic Christianity. The vision of God is the centre of religion, and the heart of faith is the conviction that communion with the living God gives life whatever significance and worth, whatever hope and mastery it may have. Without that there is no Christianity. Once emptied of vital faith in God the Church has nothing left to say to the world. It has ceased to be a constructive force at all and becomes either a picturesque anachronism (like the Lord Mayor's coach or the Bishop's gaiters) or a dead ethical traditionalism striving in vain to resist the tides of change. The first necessity for the Church today is to recover a vision of the living God. That sounds strange to many of our contemporaries whose religious awareness is no longer vivid and who therefore tend to equate Christianity with kindness, generosity and duty. But the Christian religion is, after all, not something about ourselves and our virtues ;

nor something about ourselves and our sins ; the Christian religion is something about God. Conversion lies at the heart of it and without faith in God it has no meaning.

Some, who desire a " modern " Christianity, would have it abandon its credal assertions, which seem to them the vestigial remains of a world-view that is now no longer tenable, and to identify itself frankly with the progressive ideals of humanity. But in that case it would be only another name for the ruling moral opinions of the western world. And it cannot be claimed that at the present moment these bear upon them the signs of victory. Did I not desire a " modern " Christianity I should not be at the pains of writing this book. But a religion that meets us on our own level, as a mere summary of the accepted values, must be sterile and, in the end, destructive. It may add the terrific stimulus of religion to our worst and least admirable propensities. It may only too easily become identified with the hopes and fears of a national group, thus offering dangerous reinforcement to the passions of nationalist fury. But religion is meant to redeem the social order, not to confirm it in its bad habits. Christianity preaches a gospel of redemption—of a world transformed from that which now is into the world that is willed by God, by grace of His victorious power within it. It would have no hope that can redeem the present, no faith to mould the conditions of the future, without that conviction of a living God reconciling the world to Himself, which is thought to be obscurantist and reactionary.

The attempt to substitute Man for God has brought us enough despair and confusion. There can be no true Gospel for mankind which has not the right to say to it Come up higher. There is no hope of moral emancipation except through a revival of faith in God. For the first question about Christian conduct is not What ought I to do? but What is God like? Hence the vital importance of theology. For to accept or reject Christian doctrine is not merely to entertain a preference for one possible theory as against others ; it is a decision about the way to live. It follows from this that all brave experiment in the life of the Church and in Christian practice must be guided by a secure theology. Without it we shall drift to disaster—"like waves of the sea driven by the wind and tossed, doubleminded men unstable in all our ways."

The demand for a non-theological Christianity is on the surface of it ridiculous. For what kind of religion can there be which does not involve " thinking about God "? But it really means something quite different—a theology which does not darken counsel. It is, in effect, a demand for a theology which is credible, convincing and relevant. Deeply engrained in the popular mind is the feeling that something unspecified has happened to make the traditional Christian faith untenable. People have learned the new grounds for doubt, as Dr. Matthews says, not the new grounds for confidence.[1] In actual fact, as all serious students know, contemporary movements of thought are converging upon the Christian position. The intellectual climate of our own time is far more congenial to a Theistic world-view than was that in which the

[1] *Essays in Construction*, p. 109.

Victorians grew up. But this is not yet popularly recognised. It takes something like fifty years for the work of experts in any branch of learning to percolate to the mind of the man in the street. And the popular mind is still at the mercy of views about the Christian religion and the supposed findings of science which are fifty years out of date. Christianity is believed to stand for theories about Scriptural inspiration or Miracles or everlasting punishment such as all educated Christians are in fact eager to repudiate.

Unfortunately, its intellectual mentors encourage the popular mind in these misconceptions. The Christian faith as set forth for criticism by its best-known literary opponents is often scandalously misrepresented. Even writers of scientific eminence are content to remain culpably unaware of statements of the Christian philosophy elaborated in volume after volume by men of at least their own mental calibre and often (to speak the truth) far better educated. One wonders indeed whence our " intellectuals " derive these caricatures of Christian doctrine which they demolish with such zest and brilliance. Certainly not from the Universities or from any representative Christian teacher ; hardly, one would suppose, from a pulpit. It is difficult to resist the impression that they must have relied for their information on the *obiter dicta* of the Rectory nurse-maid. The real situation now is that the best thought of the time has reached the point when only the Christian solution can rescue it from confusion and bankruptcy. There is being gradually reconstructed, by scholars and philosophers in all the Churches, an interpretation of the Universe centred upon the Christian belief in God and the Christian reading of man's life and destiny, which no other system of thought can rival. A compelling Christian theology is available, and the first duty of the Christian Church is to proclaim an intelligible religion. In religious problems (says Professor Whitehead, with his usual Delphic oracularity) " simple solutions are bogus solutions."

The Christian Church has consistently held the frontier—it is doing this already in the New Testament—against those forms of irrational emotionalism which have constantly threatened to swamp the western world. " Christianity would long ago have degenerated into a noxious superstition, apart from the levantine and European intellectual movement sustained from the very beginning until now." [1] It has sometimes been blind to new truth ; but it has never played false to reason.

It is a familiar gambit of journalism to contrast the dry, scientific light of disinterested, rational enquiry with the irrationality and obscurantism to which, it is said, the Church is committed. But that is precisely the wrong criticism. If there is an objection, it is the exact opposite—that the Church has at times cared too much for mere correctness of opinion at the risk of valuing intellectual orthodoxy above Beauty and Love, which matter more. (For if God is the Father of our Lord Jesus Christ then the Christian belief in God can never be fully contained in a formula : it is a response, a spirit and a life.) Yet the Christian creed *is* the charter

[1] *Adventures in Ideas*, p. 207.

of unfettered thought and intellectual freedom. Christianity has exalted Reason till it has enthroned it above the stars and insisted that God Himself is bound by it. We may think that its emphasis was exaggerated. We may regard the claim of the scholastics to weave the whole available sum of knowledge into a logical system of Theology as one that no sane modern man would make. Nevertheless, as Whitehead insists, it was the theology of the Western Church, with its superb and unshaken confidence in the ultimate rationality of the Universe because it is ordered by God's mind and will, which has made the triumphs of modern science possible.[1] In our day, when " a prison of the mind is being built from Strasbourg to Vladivostock,"[2] the Church still upholds the banner of freedom. It can offer people intellectual liberty because it believes in a world that does make sense, as expressed in its tremendous affirmations about the being and character of God.

Unfortunately, the traditional Christian creed has come to be bound up in its presentation with theories about the physical universe which the adult intelligence can no longer hold. Because they have abandoned the theories, people think they must cease to believe in God. Yet theories about the physical universe have been revolutionised in our lifetime : men have not ceased to believe that it exists. Belief in the existence of the external world and belief in God both depend not on any particular cosmologies, but on the pressure of recurrent experience, which

[1] *Science in the Modern World*, pp. 18, 19.
[2] *The Times*, leading article, June 21, 1934.

persists through all our changing interpretations.[1] It is not the facts, but their presentation which the advance of knowledge makes obsolete. The older theology gave the right answers to the particular questions that were put to it, and so far as they go the answers are still valid. From our point of view they were the wrong questions : or at any rate they were not the questions which the modern man wants to ask. We do not start out from the same assumptions. Our horizons are so much further distant. We conceive our world in terms of evolution and still unrealised possibilities. The ancient creeds (we say) are too small for us—though it would be hard to find a phrase more generous than the words " Creator of heaven and earth and *of all things visible and invisible.*" There is no existence, known or unknown, no depths discovered or undiscovered, which are not embraced in its magnificent outlook. But the real result of the new discoveries, with all their enlargement of our mental frontiers, is not to dethrone God from His sovereignty, but to unveil a far grander vision of the glory and majesty of the Lord.

> O Lord how glorious are thy works : thy thoughts are very deep.
> An unwise man doth not well consider this : and a fool doth not understand it.

What has broken down is not Christian faith in God, but those crude, false, unworthy ideas of Him with which we have too long limited or debased it. We cannot construct the faith of tomorrow with the mental furniture of yesterday. The dogmatic theo-

[1] *Cf.* William Adams Brown : *God at Work*, pp. 32 ff.

logies of one age are the mythological symbols of the next. We must rise to the height of God's new revelations if we would lead mankind back to conviction. Our presentation of Christian faith (in contradistinction from that faith itself) whether by way of teaching or in worship—*is* sometimes still too small and meagre to hold the allegiance of the twentieth century.[1] It is this which must now be transcended.

" The world is groping after a religion in which it can believe without evasions, without dishonest ambiguities, without self-deception and without superstition ; a religion that answers our questions not with a false completeness where completeness is impossible, but by striking to the depths within us and making us feel that those depths have been reached. . . . Above all, at this moment, a religion in which the vaster universe of modern knowledge (with all that we think we know) can be enfolded, as the universe of the middle ages (with all that they thought they knew) was organically enfolded in the religion of its intellectual leaders." [2]

Such a religion the Christian Church has ; but the case must not be allowed to go by default. Christianity will never again be strong till the Church has regained the allegiance of the educated and professional classes. We have been far too ready to assume that they are outside the scope of its ministry. Such a policy is suicidal. A terrible nemesis waits for any Church which neglects its ministry to the Universities. The close relation of Church and University has been one of the most profound influences in our national life and religion. It is

[1] " They have not revolted against the Gospel but against a presentation of the Gospel which falls far short of its true range and splendour." Lambeth *Encyclical*, 1930, p. 19.
[2] Noyes : *The Unknown God*, p. 12.

only when he travels in other countries that an English parson can fully appreciate how much this has meant both to Church and State, and how ruinous would be its severance. It is hardly too much to say that it is this educational tradition which more than anything else has saved Britain from the *Komsomol* and the *Hitler-Jugend*. At its peril will any Church forget the student-class. After all, the whole of the next generation will have its attitude to life moulded by the men and women who are today in the Colleges. If there is one suggestion which our Church may venture to offer the Church in the new countries, it is Put your picked men in your Universities. Students are a special constituency, and their needs are not satisfactorily provided for by the ordinary parochial machinery. Yet there is nothing which will count more in providing Christian leadership in the parishes as well as in education and public life. There is no cause with a stronger claim on Christians, whether in new Churches or old, than the due endowment of ministries to students.[1]

But outside this specialised area there is no less need and no less opportunity. Evangelisation in the twentieth century means primarily education, and conversion involves the allegiance of the intellect. The experience of the " Way of Renewal " has taught the clergy what liberation of spirit and what enrichment of personal devotion may come from intellectual reawakening. It has now to be transmitted to the

[1] The British Student Christian Movement is trying to establish close contacts with the parish Churches in England. Those interested should write to the Secretary of the Church of England Committee, Annandale, Golders Green, N.W. 11.

lay members. Every parish church, in its own degree
and according to the capacity of its membership,
must become a centre of Christian education. Because
we are not sufficiently alive to this immense and
exacting opportunity, we are today in very serious
danger of appealing only to the least thoughtful.
A Church which accepts that situation might as well
close down entirely. But there is a great deal of help
available. There is plenty of good and cheap literature, and an excellent scheme of group-study organised
by the B.B.C. in connexion with its religious broad-
casts. But whether by these or less formal methods, it
must be the fixed aim of the Christian pulpit to re-
capture the minds of thinking men and women, to
unveil for them anew the vision of God, and to lead
them back to a faith that stands the test. We must
disinfect Christian faith and life from the taint of any
intellectual obscurantism.

But here we must remember two facts which are
still rather imperfectly appreciated. First, that an
intelligible theology must be stated in the language
and thought-forms of the generation to which it is
addressed. Christianity, at its first appearance, had
a ready-made religious vocabulary and spoke in the
language of Jews to Jews. As it moved out into the
Roman Empire it had to create new forms of expression. The Fourth Gospel is the earliest venture, as
it is the most splendid achievement, in the re-transla-
tion of the original message into the language of a
new culture. A like task awaits our generation.
One great religious need of our own time is to find a
significant vocabulary wherein to present the eternal

and living truth in the idiom of our contemporaries. The traditional language which has been bequeathed to us from our Roman and Hellenistic inheritance no longer speaks to the twentieth-century man. Not only does it fail to convey to him the truth of which it was once the sufficient medium : it makes the quite disastrous suggestion that the Christian faith is so intertwined with the thought and life of a dead culture as to be irrelevant to his own condition.

Secondly, this fatal suggestion is reinforced by the presentation of Christian theology as an *a priori* system of doctrine unrelated to any living experience. Text-book methods are hopelessly discredited everywhere except in the teaching Church. It is high time we abandoned this anachronism. The old-fashioned deductive theology, logically consistent and impregnable, set forth, as it were, in a mental vacuum and " proved " by appeal to authoritative texts, is dangerously inadequate to the new age. The Gospel is not a theorem which can be proved by deductive argument. The proper question is not How can we prove it ? but What light does Christianity throw on life ? So, with regard to contemporary opinions, it has to be shown not that the latest pundit is prepared to concede some truth to Christianity, but that the revelation of God in Christ makes sense of the world as nothing else can. After all, the business of theology is to interpret life as men know it.

2. GOD IN CHRIST

There are, no doubt, numbers of people both within the Churches and outside them whose idea of God is still more or less formal. For them the claim that the way of revival is the way of recovered faith and vision corresponds to little in actual experience. We have first to liberate the word " God " from those suggestions of crude supernaturalism, and from those pagan and sub-Christian elements with which it is still disastrously infected. For Christianity, it must be remembered, stands for an affirmation about God uniquely and characteristically its own. Christians do not worship the Absolute, or a " numinous " cosmic emotion : still less " One above " or Old Nobodaddy : but the God and Father of our Lord Jesus Christ. And misgivings that are sometimes expressed about the implications of Christian Theism ought really to be addressed elsewhere. They are urged by able and sincere men and are entitled to a respectful answer. It is the more worth while to examine them, since the answer serves to bring out more clearly the characteristic Christian position. For in fact the objections lie much more damagingly against the philosophical and Hellenic than against the distinctively Christian form of Theism.

It is urged that belief in a God who changes not, even if purged of crude anthropomorphism, inhibits moral and intellectual enterprise : I AM is the object of a faith too static to inspire creative direction and insight in a universe of evolving ideals. But surely this is a misunderstanding ? There can be no eagerness

in the search for truth unless we believe that truth is
" there " to discover, objective, commanding and
eternal. Similarly with our moral aspirations. The
objectivity of the moral ideal is the precondition of
all free morality. We cannot base our standards and
values on a contingent and evolving goodness which
is, like ourselves, at the mercy of changing circumstances and the prey of the devouring years. It is
surely true that all spontaneity, all moral endurance
and resource, all brave research and fruitful experiment, come into life from the contemplation of the
eternal and unchanging Goodness. " Thy righteousness standeth like the strong mountains : thy judg-
ments are like the great deep." Thus belief in a God
who abides forever the same is not only (as we have
already insisted) the axiom of experimental science,
but also the inspiration of moral enterprise.

But there is something more to be said about this.
He that comes to seek Truth or Goodness must believe
not only " that it is " but that it is " the rewarder of
them that seek after it."[1] How can we be inwardly
transformed to the apprehension of that ideal which
we see from afar but leave unrealised ? It seems too
distant and inapprehensible and the very sublimity
of the far vision daunts the faltering steps with which
we approach it. The re-shaping of inward personality
cannot be achieved—it is a truism which has wrecked
many a scheme of ethics—from within that which is
to be re-made.[2]

[1] Heb. xi. 6.
[2] *Cf.* A. E. Taylor : *The Faith of a Moralist*, I, Ch. VI.,
especially p. 230.

It needs an activity brought to bear upon us by that Perfection towards which we aspire. If life is in process of becoming, if we are seeking to be transformed from the present *is* to the future *ought to be*, that can be only if the eternal Goodness is at work here within the time-process, permitting us to be made partakers of it.

It is at this point that the Christian idea of God, based on His revelation in Christ, is differentiated most clearly from the faith of the Platonic tradition. The fundamental concern of Christian Theism is with the *responsiveness* of the God it worships. It is much to know that our highest ideals have their ground in an eternal Being who is the Guarantor of our values. It is much that purified souls may contemplate them as perfected in Him. It is much, but it is not enough. For if that is all there is to be said, the hope and possibility of " salvation " remain still completely within ourselves. Man, imperfect, finite, unfinished, his spirit darkened not by ignorance only, but also by inner treachery and betrayal, has to lift himself by his own hair to the contemplation of the pure Idea and make himself partaker in the eternal. That is not specially good news for sinners. But this philosophy, even at its greatest, rests on a less than Christian idea of God. If by God we mean only Absolute Value (or as Plato would say, the Idea of Good), the problem of Nicodemus has no answer.[1] If God is but another name for a principle or ideal of perfection inaccessible to our finitude, the enigma of conscience must remain insoluble. We may worship afar, but we cannot

[1] John iii. 3-8.

" draw near " ; there is no motive power which we can supply.[1] The vision of God, in that case, may stab us with a sense of our own poverty and unworthiness, but it cannot transform us into its own likeness or admit us to redeeming communion with Him. But if God is the Father of our Lord Jesus Christ, if He is (as Christians say) " Love," then He is self-revealing, self-communicating, imparting to His creatures His own excellence and redeeming men's hearts by the grace of Christ—filling the earth with majesty and wonder.

This is what matters to the religious man. His concern is not with abstract speculation but with the character of the God he worships. To believe in God is of little importance unless He is the living Redeemer as well as the ground of Goodness and Reality. If it is otherwise, faith in God is mainly a matter of academic interest. It could not make much moral difference. A God who merely accounts for the world as it is—whether as the Eternal Mathematician, the Supreme Value, the Infinite Being, or whatever other concepts men may form of Him—is not a God whom Christians can worship. He does not fulfil the law of Christ. Christianity requires the conviction of a God who is Transformer and Redeemer, who is Himself the Giver of all Goodness and the Source of the faith by which we move towards Him. Thus God meets us " in the face of Christ." What is distinctive about Christian Theism is the mediation of God to man through Him.

[1] *Cf.* " No man comes to me except God the Father draw him " side by side with " No man comes to the Father but by me."

Dr. Oman's magnificent volume *The Natural and the Supernatural* has made clear how close is the connexion between a true Christian theology and a true theory of knowledge. And, in fact, in all our experience there is at least an element of response to initiative which is brought to bear upon us. All growth, whether physical or spiritual, involves some reciprocal relationship between us and the sustaining environment. Knowledge is the reply to a question which is asked as much by the known as by the knower.[1] That mysterious fact which we describe as " influence " is a movement upon us from another, and not *from* another only, but *through* him. There are people to whom, as we say, we " owe our souls." Are we not conscious that through those men and women something comes out of the heart of things, revealing to us more than *their* character—a quality of life and spirit which we know to have a claim upon us, and summoning us to move out and meet it ? We learn from these familiar examples that Reality is self-communicating and, at least in some of its modes, redemptive. The Saints and the classic personalities in religion, conduct and the arts exemplify this fact still more significantly. In Christ the principle is fulfilled. In Him that comes forth to meet us which we know to be sovereign and absolute.

---

[1] " Both chronologically and causally, the act of perception starts at the end of the chain remote from the percipient—in the sun, the electric light or the chair. We must not, for instance, compare the act of vision, as Descartes did, to a poking about in space as a blind man pokes about with a stick ; the object is the starting point not the terminus of an act of perception." Sir J. Jeans : *The New Background of Science*, p. 11.

It is God and no other who there lays His touch
upon us. It is this decisive Christian experience,
verified, possessed and interpreted by His work upon us
in Christ Jesus, which creates conviction in a redeeming God. The response which God through Christ
evokes from us teaches us to hear his invitation in the
pressure upon us of all claims of goodness, and then
to move out in Christian faith and worship over the
whole wide range of values.

In an earlier book, I wore out my readers in
attempting to answer the question What are values ?
The answer was not completely satisfactory ; but I
think now that it was the wrong question. It belongs
to a different philosophy. The right approach, as I
am now suggesting, is the very much more direct
question What kind of God do Christians worship ?
All the rest will flow from our answer to it. But it
must be recognised frankly that this approach
leads us along a road on which Christianity
and Platonism cannot for long be travelling com-
panions.

This has been very strongly urged recently by the
Swedish theologian, Dr. Nygren, in his study *Eros
and Agape*. He desires to establish a sharp distinction
between Christianity and Platonism as seen in their
respective ideas of Love. He rightly insists that the
Greek *Eros*, even its most spiritualised form, even in the
great Platonic *Symposium*, remains something essentially man-centred. It is the eternal spark in the
human soul, imprisoned here in " becoming " and
delusion, aspiring to rise towards the eternal Forms
and reunite with the eternal reality. The initiative

is with the ascending soul, not in the Goodness towards which it aspires. There is no equivalent to the idea of " Grace," of the self-impartation of infinite to finite. Even in its development in Aristotle, for whom God is the cause of all " movement "—advance from lower to higher realisation in the rational hierarchy of the Universe—as the object of the world's desire (κινεῖ ὡς ἐρώμενον), there is no place for any divine initiative. It cannot be said that God loves the world, of whose existence He cannot be aware since He contemplates only His own rationality. There is no equivalent to the Christian saying We love, because He first loved us.

But the whole Christian conception of Love—and the point, he thinks, of some of the hardest parables such as that of the Labourers in the Vineyard—is that all love has its source in God, not in anything of intrinsic worth in man. (" While we were yet sinners Christ died for us.") So that what Christianity intends by *Agape* is the exact contradictory of *Eros*. It means partaking in that divine life imparted to us by its divine Source, admitting us to participation in it. Thus the idea of the " worth of the human soul " is a pagan not a Christian conception. All that is lovable in us is of God's gift ; and the love which is characteristic of the New Testament is entirely and wholly a God-given " Grace." Christians are moved to love of the brethren because God through Christ has visited and enabled them—simply and solely because God *is* love. The two conceptions are strictly antithetical. Dr. Nygren quotes the dictum of Williamowitz that, if the author of 1 Cor.

xiii. and Plato could meet one another, despite the
similarity of their language they would find no point
in common.

He therefore suggests that the whole Platonic
tradition in Christian theology is a mistake.   It was
Luther's outstanding achievement, he thinks, to call the
Church back from the Hellenic categories which it had
used as its theological medium to its own native and
characteristic emphasis on the knowledge of God
through " Grace " by faith alone.

Dr. Nygren, I think, overstates his case.   These
sharp, absolute antitheses are almost bound to fail
to do justice to the complex history of ideas.   Plato's
philosophy is majestic witness to the hunger and thirst
of man for the eternal ;   and unless there is that in
the soul of man which is there depicted as *Eros*, is it
true that man is " made in the image of God," or
would any incarnation be possible ?   We must also
insist on a further qualification.   True as it is, and
as has been urged already, that the primary and
essential Christian emphasis is its faith in God as
Redeemer lifting men to share in His own perfection,
yet an exclusive emphasis on redemption, overlooking
God's work in creation, is at once intellectually
unsatisfying and also fatal to any Christian ethic.
To this we return at further length subsequently.
Meanwhile, it seems relevant to remind ourselves that
Luther's achievement has another side to it.   Without
realising its disastrous consequences, he did in effect
withdraw Christianity from all those values of
humanist culture of which the *philosophia perennis* of
the mediæval Church was the vehicle.   He repudiated

more than St. Thomas ; he abandoned the hope of
transforming the world. The subsequent history of
the Protestant Churches, wavering in unstable equili-
brium between pietism and secularisation, may serve
both as commentary and warning.

These reservations must be made first. Nevertheless, with all these qualifications, Dr. Nygren's
thesis is of the greatest importance. In the last resort,
as it seems to me, the Christian and the Platonic forms
of Theism are not only different, but incompatible.
" Speaking as a theist " (writes Dr. Inge)[1] " I
regard religion as an affirmation and apprehension
of absolute values." But this, surely, is not the
Christian starting-point. Speaking as a Christian, I
regard religion as an act of trust and self-committal
to the God and Father of our Lord Jesus Christ.
Faith in absolute values is quite possible without
having heard so much as the name of Christ. His
place in the " platonic " theology is that of a uniquely
impressive witness to an independently valid body of
truth, which would still remain credible without Him.
And there are, certainly, very many roads which lead
men to the knowledge of the true God : but no man
comes to the Father but by Him. There is no direct
path from " absolute values " to the Christian belief
in God. Metaphysically, it is just possible to employ
the philosophy of values as the vehicle of Christian
theology ; some well-known and deservedly esteemed

---

[1] *God and the Astronomers*, p. 175. For a damaging but constructive criticism of Platonism as a " religion of escape " and
therefore sub-Christian, see L. W. Grensted, *The Person of Christ*,
p. 180.

books are the evidence that it can be done. Yet when
we come to religion and morality, the whole tone and
temper of this philosophy breathes in a climate which
is not that of the Gospels. It could never be claimed
of absolute values that they come to seek and to save
that which is lost. It cannot be said of Beauty, Truth
and Goodness that they " take upon themselves man
to deliver him." The Platonic God could become
incarnate only at the price of ceasing to be God.
In practice no less than in speculation we seem to
encounter this incompatibility. There is something in
the Platonic tradition, however nobly and generously
interpreted, which remains aristocratic and exclusive.
Now and again it degenerates into scorn. " This
multitude which knoweth not the values. . . ." But
the Christian religion, when all is said and done, is
not the ascent of purified souls to the contemplation
of the absolute values : it is the response of the
common man and sinner to God's redeeming and self-
revealing activity. The absolute values are not *alive :*
they are metaphysical and moral concepts.

We are getting near to the centre of our enquiry.
For this reason I am specially anxious that the next
stages in the argument should not be dismissed as
abstract and " highbrow," and that I should succeed
in making them intelligible. For if I succeed, it is
upon these positions that the whole presentation of
the Christian Church and of the content of the
Christian life which is contained in these chapters
rests.

The idea of absolute values belongs to that " intel-
lectualist " Greek philosophy of which, to its own

constant embarrassment, the Christian Church became legatee. This system seeks to interpret the Universe in terms of static, conceptual perfection, and assumes that what is most real and most akin to the divine nature is that which approximates most closely to the order of pure conceptual selfconsistency. In other words, that is most divine which is most completely impersonal and furthest removed from any such contingency as is implied in a living, personal will. It requires elaborate mental acrobatics to square these philosophical assumptions with the personalist and experimental approach to the interpretation of our experience which is congenial to the twentieth century. It is still more difficult to harmonise them with the presuppositions of Jesus Christ, and that faith in a " personal," living God which we inherit, through Him, from Judaism. They belong to a different tradition. Christianity is irrevocably committed to faith in a God active in the world, the creative Source of all that is good in it, the Conqueror of what is evil. Nothing is Christian which obscures that emphasis. This, as we have seen, is consistent with all our experience of reality in the various modes of its presentation to us. But for Christians the decisive experience is the impact of Spirit on our spirits which is mediated through Jesus Christ. He is central, the unique mediator. And what gives Christian Theology its breadth, its range and its generous humanism, is just this centrality of Christ in authentic Christian experience. We know that God is at work in the world because we know what He does through Christ. In Him we know God as Redeemer, and this experience of the Holy Spirit is the guarantee of faith in a living God, imparting to the world His own excellence and evoking from it ever new responses.

This saving knowledge of God through Jesus Christ is at once more intimate and more significant than any other moments in our knowledge of Him.

The living heart of Christian conviction is the incomparable and unique preciousness of His work in man's life through Christ, giving us the right to become sons of God, pardoning, sanctifying and renewing, and eliciting out of common human nature still undisclosed possibilities. In the great picture in the Sistine chapel, the touch of God on man's sleeping spirit is summoning Adam into life. On those who will respond to Christ's call the touch is more intimate and life-giving, and it makes them free of a new world of experience. God's greatest work in human nature is made possible because of Christ. Where frightened and sinful men and women dare through Christ to say " Abba, Father " ; where they are made partakers of His Spirit and gathered into that redeeming intimacy ; there is an activity of God towards us so decisive in its depth and richness as to be almost incommensurable with His other acts and self-disclosures. It is the unique and characteristic instance of God's responsiveness to the needs of men. If that is blurred, we have lost Christianity. *Compared with this* all other modes of God's activity and self-revelation are for us at least relatively secondary. Where men see Christ as central in the Universe they commit themselves to an affirmation in the light of which all their other insights, as well as all their critical reservations, become relatively unimportant.

Now this perhaps is what underlies the traditional theological distinction between Natural and Supernatural. In the forms in which it has hitherto been stated, few modern thinkers will wish to defend it. To the man in the street the word "supernatural" stands for a crude conception of the miraculous ; and when he says that he cannot accept a supernatural form of Christianity this is probably what he has in mind. In fact, what he is really repudiating is not Christianity, but Deism. Yet even in its philosophical form, in its Thomist and scholastic formulation, the distinction seems to most of us untenable. Few today, outside the Roman communion, could endorse the metaphysic on which it rests or the concept of God which it implies. We cannot accept this hard and fast Dualism. There is one world, we say, and the world is God's. So we tend to say, in loose, popular language, " everything is equally supernatural "—a statement which may be justified as a protest against a crude, uncriticised supernaturalism, but is, nevertheless, quite inadequate to the realities of Christian experience.

For the distinction does stand for something. In itself, the word " supernatural " has become so deeply involved in false and misleading associations that Theology would be wise to abandon it. But we cannot escape from what it stands for.

In the book to which I have already referred, Dr. Oman finds that the " supernatural " is the

self-disclosing Reality which is the constant
presupposition of all our knowledge and all our
experience. Thus all growth in wisdom and
stature is indeed " supernaturally " imparted to us.
It is, I fear, almost impertinent to refer thus briefly,
in passing, to a treatise of such far-reaching importance.
But I do not believe that, in the long run, we can
wholly dispense with the distinction which the older
theologies recognised. If we could find the right way
of stating it, must we not maintain that there was
" something in it " ? The intellectual forms in which
it was stated are, admittedly, tenable no longer.
Von Hugel, all through his massive studies, was
wrestling with an attempt at re-statement. There
are few, probably, who can feel quite certain either
that they have understood his position or, if they have,
that they find it quite satisfying. But the instinct of
the Church was probably right. For the Church
itself and the Christian life *are* " other "—not " wholly
other," but nevertheless " other "—than anything
else in human experience. The revelation of God
through Christ Jesus *is* something different and
distinct from the revelation of God through a sunset—
though it is the same God who is revealed. It is
what constitutes Christianity ; and this was what the
traditional statements meant by God's supernatural
gifts to man. That, I suggest, is what the distinction
stood for. It stood for the real difference in quality
between God's activity in the world as the Source of
all Truth and Goodness and that most inward,
characteristic work in us which has been made possible
by Christ Jesus.

This is in agreement with the New Testament.
The Epistles and Gospels never doubt that the Spirit
of God is at work in the pagan conscience and in
whatsoever is honest, true and lovely : yet they are
almost ruthless in insisting that God's gift through
Christ—the Holy Spirit—is at once the essential
endowment and the unique prerogative of Christians. It is right that we should school our minds to
recognise and worship the divine glory in the vastness
and majesty of the Universe, in all worth-while forms
of activity, and in all that is wonderful and praise-
worthy. But it is possible for our thought of God to
become so generalised and impersonal that the heart
of the believer remains cold and is never kindled into
communion with Him. And indeed it seems that a
certain homeliness in the approach of the worshipper
to God is necessary to the Christian religion. The
doctrinal and liturgical tradition of the Church as
the family of worshippers is peculiarly adapted to
that need. It comes to God " through Jesus Christ."
Its central and almost exclusive emphasis is upon
this act and revelation : and in other modes of God's
work in the world it seems, by comparison, to have
little interest.

Now this is both a strength and a weakness.
The parson who said " I cannot understand what
cosmic processes have to do with religion " was
technically, of course, professing Arianism—though
he would have been horrified to know this.
But he had a case, all the same. The Church is
here to proclaim what it knows—that God redeems
man through Jesus Christ, and to keep open that

central gateway through which men come to the knowledge of the Father. That is its primary task and its chief business. Its massive liturgical concentration—with the almost total exclusion from its worship of any response to the divine activity in the broad fields of life as a whole outside His work in man through the Incarnation—is the sign of its fidelity to that trust. It is right in its instinctive recognition that if it extends its line on too wide a front it may find its centre and citadel exposed. There is, however, a danger lest by refusing to establish contacts it may find itself in a perilous isolation.

It is right that Christians should be recalled from vague, nebulous ideas of God to a " Christocentric " theology. But, as I have tried elsewhere to point out, this fundamental Christian insistence is always in danger of being isolated from the other factors in human experience. Religion is then left in a vacuum, unrelated to those tasks and claims and those other forms of activity and knowledge which are the actual substance of human life. Then religion is left high and dry, and seems irrelevant to the world of affairs. It cannot hope to transform the social order or even to have any great importance for it, unless we relate the knowledge of God in Christ with the actual business of living in the world, and the needs, interests and opportunities of contemporary civilisation. But if we know God through Jesus Christ, we know Him both as Redeemer and Creator ; and we know that what He achieves in the hearts of men and women because of Him, it is His will to achieve throughout the whole world.

3. CREATOR AND REDEEMER

The Object of Christian faith and worship is the God and Father of our Lord Jesus Christ. They remain on a sub-Christian level till they have reached, through Christ, to the Father, the Creator both of heaven and earth. The Christian religion must therefore have a place within the range of its doctrine and devotion for other concerns in life than the religious. If it is God who meets us in Christ, then our response to all forms of Goodness—in thought, appreciation or conduct—is bound up with our response to Him and is part of a Christian's conversion. To this conviction we are committed by the Christology of the Fourth Gospel and the classical Christian theology. It is taken for granted in the catholic creeds. The God who is known to us in Christ is not only the Object of religion : He is the living reality of the world. If Christ is " of one essence " with the Father, then the Universe is committed to Him ; in Him the purpose immanent in history emerges into personal embodiment ; in Him uniquely we have access to the creative and redemptive forces which are alive at the heart of our experience. The God and Father of our Lord Jesus Christ is known to us, through Him, with a special inwardness ; no man comes to the Father but by Him. But God does not live in the sacristy. He is not the monopoly of Christians. He is the Creator of the world ; and the will which is incarnate in Christ is His will for the world of His creating. It is therefore not the religion of Christians which leaves the world unredeemed behind it. " The true way of redemption from ' the world ' is the way of reconciliation to the purposes of God in the world." Nor is it a Christian theology which excludes from its field of vision the activity of God in the world apart from and outside of the Incarnation   It is, indeed, the heresy of Arius.   The " Nicene " creed is 'a standing protest against committing ourselves to a Redeemer who is not truly " one " with the Creator. For that breaks our inner life into fragments.

But this is, as it seems to me, the weak point in the so-called Barthian theology which is sweeping the continental Universities and beginning to exercise an influence on the theological faculties in England. It has been its great and massive contribution to recover the sense of the divine initiative.   Christianity, it insists, starts with God and His redemptive activity towards us, not with our wavering " ideals " or the temperature of our religious emotions. God, says Barth, is the Subject of theology, and all our knowledge of Him derives from the utterance of His Word revealed in us, which at once breaks us and liberates us.   But (apart from the fact that not all Christian experience is, or ought to be, of this " twice-born " type) just how is God's word revealed ? For if God is known to us only in religion, and the specifically religious responses, then the knowledge of God is confined to this one form of our experience. It is hard, in that case, to see how the knowledge of God can unify life into a coherent whole or redeem and sanctify its manifold enterprises. If it cannot do this, it is stultified. Moreover, as I have elsewhere insisted, if religion is thus drawn apart from life it becomes itself impoverished and anæmic. But it is precisely into this impasse that the Barthian theology seems to be leading us.

The moral grandeur of Karl Barth's resistance to the force of the totalitarian State makes it a most unwelcome task to criticise him. Yet we cannot accept his theology.

For Barth, so far as I understand him, seems to desire to establish a sharp distinction between the faith by which God is apprehended and all the other activities of our spirits. It is something unique and incommensurable ; when the visitation comes to men they recognise it. But what of those who remain unvisited by these apocalyptic disclosures ? They are, after all, the majority of mankind. All such attempts at isolating religion in order to vindicate its reality result, in the end, in leaving " religious experience " too much at the mercy of our moods and tenses. Notoriously this has been the consequence of attempts to interpret the nature of religion by analytic and psychological methods. Though Barthianism starts from the other end, and is rigorously *a priori*, it cannot be said to succeed in avoiding this danger.

The difficulty is more than a matter of method : it concerns the being and nature of God. Barth is concerned to recall Christianity to the prophetic and biblical tradition and recover its lost faith in a living God. That is a wholly legitimate ambition, as has been strongly urged in the previous pages. The God of Jeans, Eddington and Whitehead seems to be a long way removed from the God of Abraham,

Isaac and Jacob. But this leads Barth to distinguish abruptly between the revelation of God in the Bible and any other relative apprehension of Him. God is known to us through the prophets and through His Word incarnate in Christ. There is no other authentic revelation to which faith can make its response.

No doubt we are prone, in preaching, to imply that ; and the strongly biblical colouring of our liturgies and the massing of historical suggestions intended to evoke faith and worship may tend to impose it upon congregations. But to this Christianity cannot give its sanction. It is not consistent with its own creed. Still less can it endorse the attempt to enhance the glory of God's redemption by denigration of the natural man. " The power of God (writes Barth) can be detected neither in the world of nature nor in the souls of men."[1] But if God is in no sense revealed in the glory and majesty of the world and the plain goodness of common men and women—their cheerfulness, their patience and their courage—then Christianity is a mistake. For then God is not at work in the world in any such sense as the Gospel claims.

Vital religion can never be safeguarded by rending the texture of man's experience. Barthianism is really another form of that dualism between faith and knowledge, reason and revelation, which has haunted Protestant Christianity and is fast draining it of its vitality. It is indeed scarcely less disastrous than the dualism between cultus and ethics which has vitiated some forms of Catholicism. It is, moreover, completely at variance with the attitude expressed in the Parables,

[1] *Epistle to the Romans*, p. 36.

with their serene, majesterial confidence that the world is God's world and He is at work in it, so that His revelations in nature and history are solid with His disclosures in religion, and the laws that govern the manifold life of men are, at their own level and in their own degree, manifestations of the Father's will.[1] Christianity is profoundly committed to this faith in God as Creator of the world no less than the Redeemer of man's life. The two conceptions are obviously indissoluble. If God is not the Lord of the Universe He cannot give us victory in the world but only provide a means of escape from it—and that is not Christianity, but paganism. Undeniably the Christian Gospel has been presented in that form at some periods, and the Church today is still paying the price. Therefore we owe a deep gratitude to Professor Raven for his vehement and tenacious reminders that God is the Creator of the Universe and that religion is only significant in the context of our experience as a whole.

Nevertheless, this necessary insistence is also exposed to its own particular dangers. Disinterested search for truth, self-sacrificing love or devotion to duty, are genuine responses to the claim of God, even though men are not consciously aware of Him, even though they profess themselves atheists. At all costs we must hold fast to that. Yet the fact remains that, though these attitudes may be in themselves profoundly " religious," they cannot be identified with religion. The knowledge of God which is given through religion is not a more reliable form of know-

[1] *Cf.* O. C. Quick : *The Realism of Christ's Parables.*

H

ledge than that which comes through Science, Art or Morality—all true knowledge is knowledge of the true God. But it has a real difference in its quality. It has a depth, inwardness and richness, a cleansing and lifegiving vitality which is its own inalienable prerogative. Moreover, human experience on a wide scale seems to show that all those activities which belong to what we recognise as the good life lack something in strength and creativity and may even become sterile and degenerate when they are not fructified by religion and brought consciously into relation to God. And if man is indeed made for communion with God this is just what we should expect. So long as his deepest need is unsatisfied (though he may not himself be aware of it), there is a frustration in his inner life ; his full possibilities remain unrealised, his richest gifts still unevoked, and it happens sometimes that his best " goes bad on him." (That some atheists are far finer characters than some Christians is plainly not an objection to this statement.) He needs both fulfilment and redemption in that conscious response to God, as the Object of worship, faith and consecration, which is the concern of religion.

Further than this, while we must maintain that every recognition of goodness is a real disclosure of God, yet if we accustom ourselves to thinking as though God's revelation in a sunset is on an equality and on the same level with His revelation in Christ Jesus—we have parted company with the Christian religion. The salt will be found to have lost its saltness, the distinctive savour has gone. What is at issue here is something far more than the distinction between persons and things, and the obvious fact that a personal revealer can disclose God more fully than an impersonal. It is the core and essence of Christianity. The God whom the Christian Church proclaims is the God who redeems us through Jesus Christ ; and He is the Redeemer and the Mediator. To obscure or minimise the uniqueness and centrality of Christ in Christianity is to change it into a different religion.

But God is the Creator of the world, and we cannot isolate His work through Christ from His other creative and redemptive activity, and the other modes of His self-disclosure. All the divine activity in the world, so far at least as concerns man— and that is all that religion can respond to—is at once creative and redemptive. His every disclosure to our sleeping spirits, whether on the peaks of heroic insight or the pedestrian walks of daily duty, whether in the achievement of new knowledge, in the mastery of technical skill, in the opening of our hearts to love and beauty, or through the conviction of forgiveness, comes to us as summons and awakening, inviting us to communion with Himself. If God is indeed the living God, ceaselessly imparting to the world His own original, underived excellence, then all loyal response to goodness, in whatever forms it may be presented to us, is genuine response to God. All goodness is of the divine initiative. It is not of ourselves, it is the gift of God—" in his majesty as Creator and his even greater majesty as Redeemer." [1] But

1 *Cf.* Lambeth *Encyclical*, 1930, p. 20.

Creator and Redeemer are one God. He meets us " in all that calls forth the reverence and admiration of men and women at their best," in the glory of nature, in the commands of conscience, and most characteristically yet most searchingly in His revelation " in the face of Christ." The so-called secular tasks and interests are bound up with the religion of a Christian. Intellectual and æsthetic values are part of God's gift and revelation to Him. But only because of the outflow upon them of that faith in God's revealing and redeeming work which is mediated for him by Christ. It is out of the matrix of this experience that the Christian concern with " the values " is born.

To this experience the Church exists primarily in order to bear witness. It is an " otherworldly " society of men " not conformed to this world." But it is this in order that the world and the whole of man's thought and enterprise may be gathered within God's redemptive purpose and brought into conformity with His will.

A true theology therefore we must have. Without it all the activity of the Church will be misdirected or insecure. But worship moulds the theology of its members, and exhibits it to the world, far more effectively, both for good and evil, than any formulation of doctrine. It is through the worship of the Christian Society and the spiritual quality of its life that the vision of God in His majesty and glory is to be manifested among men.

CHAPTER IV

THE RENAISSANCE OF WORSHIP

1. THE THEOLOGY OF WORSHIP

IN times of public anxiety like the present, there is always the cry What is the Church *doing?* The most obvious thing that the Church does, what every onlooker can watch it doing, is to gather people together for worship. And this is not only its most obvious, but its most characteristic activity. The Church is a community of worshippers, and the worship of God is its primary concern. At every level, primitive or developed, worship is the hall-mark of religion. Till recently this would have been such a platitude that it would not have been worth while to say it. Today it sounds almost paradoxical. In the past, perhaps, we may have been too ready to think that the Church was discharging its mission so long as its buildings were filled with worshippers, and, obviously, a Church may be full and yet have little to do with Christianity. But we have reacted against this so violently and have been so eager to insist that " Church-going is not the whole of religion " that it almost needs courage to suggest now that " going to Church " really is important. Start-ling though it may be, we must risk saying so. For when we have made every qualification, it remains true that the influence of the Church depends upon the quality of its worship—which is not only its primary means of grace, but also its chief instrument of evangelism and its most vital contribution to the Christianisation of the social order. Its revival in England depends, more than on any other one factor, on a renaissance in Christian public worship. " The younger generation is not very much interested in theological dogma and it is almost wholly uninterested in principles of Church Government. What it is concerned about in the sphere of organised religion is to find a cult which is spiritually satisfying." [1]

When we think of the rather lifeless congregations sometimes found in our Churches and Cathedrals—only too frequently a tiny handful gathered out of a vast population—we cannot but feel that something has gone wrong. Is this what the Church claims chiefly to be doing? Is it a very important contribution to the anxious life of the twentieth century? Admittedly it is possible for worship to be as deadly as anything imaginable, and utterly deadening in its effects. Everyone with his eyes open knows that. I do not think we could honestly be surprised if few of the rising generation were prepared to regard Services in Church as an integral part of their Christian lives.

Yet if the habit of public worship dies out the Church and the Christian ethic will die with it. Before all else, the Christian community is a fellowship united by worship of the God and Father of our Lord Jesus Christ. That is its essential bond of unity.

[1] Micklem : *Our Approach to God*, p. 11.

We have seen how deep it lies in the Christian view of things that the Grace of God is offered and secured to us through the common faith and worship of the society. And if Christians do not share together in this central and primary religious experience, can they remain a community at all? It was the need of the Church for large buildings in which its congregations could meet —by contrast with the small pagan temples in which the priests were to offer sacrifice—which has filled the world with the glorious architecture which still remains to the twentieth-century man the chief visible symbol of religion.

Moreover, most of the forces of the modern world conspire to make belief in God difficult. When we think of the pressure of materialism, the strength of worldly and trivial suggestion, the despair-laden atmosphere of scepticism which weigh on the spirit of the modern man, how can we hope that people will resist them or retain their hold on spiritual conviction apart from the focus of public worship and the illumination and renewal of which it should be the God-given vehicle? Men will sit starving in the midst of plenty, trying to keep alive an impoverished and often devitalised religion with their own meagre insight and experience. By participation in corporate worship they may be made free of a range and richness of spiritual conviction and experience far exceeding anything accessible to the lonely search of an individual faith.

Yet to deplore the poverty of Church-going is a rather futile proceeding. It is a barren and negative approach. We shall not secure a revival of worship by bleating entreaties to the young to "come to Church" as a painful Christian duty, still less by devising artful dodges which may attract them inside our Churches. We need far more constructive remedies. To invite people to come to Church is useless unless we are giving more thought and trouble to what they are to find when they get there. For at present far too many are being starved. Many have ceased to hope that the Churches can satisfy their instinctive need for worship, and must either allow the instinct to wither or seek elsewhere an inferior satisfaction for it in dancing, pageantry, tattoos, and even the crude emotional "kick" of the cinema—which at least takes people out of themselves a little, though it may not take them to God. The Church cannot regain its leadership till it regains the capacity for worship. This cannot be done by mere rule of thumb. It demands acknowledged, creative principles and a clear apprehension both of what, as worshippers, we are trying to do and of what we expect to receive. It needs a solid theological background and a power of imaginative interpretation.

The odd thing is that so little thought is devoted to this exceedingly urgent task. There is plenty of first-class constructive thinking in the re-presentation of creeds and theology, and an output of administrative ability which may fairly be claimed as of "cabinet rank." On the crucial question of worship in the circumstances of the twentieth century mostly flabby thought is being expended. "The defect of the liberal theology of the last two hundred years— wrote Dr. Whitehead—is that it has confined itself to the suggestion of minor vapid reasons why people should continue to go to Church in the traditional fashion." [1]   This is really the crux of the whole situation.   A true and vital theology is necessary ; but it will not win the allegiance of the new age unless expressed and interpreted in worship.   We labour to bring our theology up to date in the changed mental climate of our own time, but assume that traditional worship just " goes on."   In point of fact, it is not going on, and such experiments as are being made are too often erratic and uninformed.   We cannot go farther till we have thought more.   If public worship is lifeless and mechanical, if (as may be true in extreme instances) it is even detrimental to religion, this may be partly because modern Christians have as a rule so few clear conceptions of the nature and meaning of worship itself.   Why do we worship and what are we trying to do ?

Worship begins, as it ends, in wonder.   In essence it is the outreach of man to the spiritual factor in his environment, in which alone his life is fulfilled.   It may thus be said to be natural to man, and, in fact, we find no stage in history at which man has not been a worshipper.   Even at its most primitive level, where it may not amount to very much more than a dim recognition of the uncanny, it has nevertheless a coercive quality.   The object of worship is always regarded as exercising a claim on the worshipper, and therefore as *sacred* rather than merely odd.   Thus worship starts (as Dr. Kirk says), not in any activities of our own, but in those which God brings to bear upon

[1] *Adventures of Ideas*, p. 208.

us.[1] Thus, as in the order of nature, all growth and all advance in knowledge are by way of *response* to environment, so it is that in the realm of spirit we grow in grace and in the knowledge of God. What religion calls the offering of worship is, in fact, our response to that touch of God on our hearts and minds which is what it calls Grace. Worship and Grace are always correlative, as action and contemplation are correlative. It is God who evokes the response which He rewards. We must no doubt be prepared to recognise as manifestations of the spirit of worship man's many and various responses to the claim of the spiritual upon him—in submission to the imperatives of conscience, disinterested devotion to knowledge, surrender to the vision of beauty, in the lover's self-dedication, and all other recognitions of worth. But the specifically religious consciousness learns to hear in and through these the call of the infinite Perfection summoning spirit to its true fulfilment where alone it can be wholly satisfied. It knows that in response to this claim it finds the fulfilment of its own nature in personal communion with God. There we have worship in its true meaning.

For Christians it means even more than this. Worship, in its Christian definition, is the hallowing of God's name. This is the end for which man was

[1] " Worship depends not upon our own activities but upon the activities which God brings to bear upon us ; to them we are forced to react as worshippers. If without selfscrutiny and selftorment a man can remain alive to the goodness in his environment, it will draw out all that is best in him, leading him ever nearer to the perfect goodness revealed in the Incarnate Lord." Kirk : *The Vision of God*, p. 465.

created—to glorify God and enjoy Him for ever.
Thus in extent it is as wide as life.   For it covers both
the direct approach to God in prayer, sacrament and
adoration, and all those activities of spirit which are
called forth, sustained and redeemed by our response
to the vision of God in Christ.   The life of spirit needs
for its full development both the rest of contempla-
tive enjoyment and the energy of active response.
Christian worship embraces both these moments.
In both these aspects it is the gift of God.   But it is the
gift of God in a unique sense.   The true differentia of
Christian worship is that it is the response of man's spirit
to God's special grace and revelation mediated through
Jesus Christ.   Its inmost shrine is communion with
Him in the gracious and forgiving love wherein
Christ reveals Him as Father.

The life of spirit is all of one piece, and worship
ought to redeem and fructify all those responses
to Spirit which God through Christ evokes and
rewards.   The vision of God in Christ is continuous
with the vision of God in His other modes of self-
manifestation and self-giving, which at once sustain
and are enriched by it.   In all such visitations and
influences the Holy Spirit invites our response to
the God and Father of our Lord Jesus Christ.   If
Christ is the true Light that lighteth every man, then
whatever is good and true and lovely is the gift and
the invitation of the Father, summoning us to communion with Himself.   It ought, therefore, to go
without saying that all appreciation of value, in whatever form it may be presented to us, is a true hallowing
of God's name and a true concern of Christian wor-

shippers. Where men are making goodness come true—whether in thought, in act, or in conduct—there they are setting forward God's glory. If to worship is to hallow God's name, then one intention of religious worship is that men should glorify God in those other activities of life which are not specifically religious.

But all Christian experience seems to show that such continual "living in God's presence," such dedication of thought and will to Him, need direct communion with God in prayer. Neglect of the latter gravely impoverishes and normally even rules out the former. Further than this, the full liberation and sanctification of Christian faith and prayer is the fruit of that unique experience which is open to us in corporate Christian worship.

Our concern in this chapter is limited to this corporate public worship of Christians—that is, to " Services " in church. The private devotions of individual Christians, the family worship of the Christian home, and the prayer-meeting of friends and associates derive from and are dependent on the corporate worship of Christ's society. Moreover, the intimacy and informality proper to such occasions of worship obviously differ in quality from that which inheres in corporate public worship.

It is true, no doubt, that there are many Christians who would find it hard to endorse, from their own experience, the exalted claim we have made for corporate worship. Its deepest and richest possibilities may be revealed, or they may be obscured, by the ways in which such worship is presented. A truly interpretative presentation presupposes a right understanding as well as the art to evoke the essential experience.

It is one of the aims of this chapter to set out the significance of Christian worship in its widest range of interpretation. But that which constitutes Christianity is the unique work of God in man by His manifestation "in the face of Christ," and the gift which is shared in the redeemed community. It is this which is at the centre of Christian worship, and the characteristic " response " of Christians is towards that uniquely redemptive act. By comparison all else is secondary.

We cannot doubt, therefore, that the Church is right in its massive concentration, in worship, on the facts unique to Christian experience—Grace, Forgiveness, Reconciliation, the joyful acceptance of the Gospel, the offering of ourselves " through Jesus Christ " and newness of life through the Resurrection. What God achieves in the life of men through Christ *is* " other " than what He achieves or can achieve in lives in which Christ is not enthroned. To doubt that is to doubt Christianity. And thus—quite apart from the question of its supposed Dominical Institution, into which we cannot here enter—the Eucharist or Holy Communion Service is the norm and archetype of the worship of Christians. Within that experience of worship the Christian is in his true native climate. When disciples meet in the name of Christ, not trusting in their own righteousness, to submit themselves to His redeeming influence and to offer themselves through Him to the Father, there they know a Presence in the midst of them, and a new life released in their hearts which is unique in its inwardness and richness. This is, indeed, the crucial vindication of God's responsiveness to the needs of men. All that Christian devotion means by " Grace " is dependent upon this unique experience.

But those who have understood this most vividly have often dangerously misinterpreted it. Christians believe in the Real Presence of the living Christ in the Eucharist because they believe in His Presence in the Church. It has been too often stated the other way round, as though the ground for believing in the Church is the gift that comes through the Eucharist —which is Counter-Reformation Theology. This is more than an academic point ; it affects our whole conception of worship and of the method of God's work in men. This error is but another form of that false interpretation of Christ (technically called the Eutychian heresy) which was rejected in the fifth century. Overwhelmed by the sense that through Jesus Christ God Himself touches the lives of men, by the " given-ness " of Grace and truth through Him, it presented Him as a kind of impersonal instrument through which God's redemptive work was done, not a Person compact of emotion, thought and will. But that would have made of Him a mere channel through which an influence of redemption flowed, not a living, personal Redeemer. That would have left God's work in Christ unique indeed, but totally unrelated to anything else in human experience or to His claim on the reason and will of men. It would have made " salvation " impersonal—which is inconsistent with Christianity.

There is too much teaching about the " Real Presence " which is perilously akin to this heresy. It treats the Sacraments as a kind of pipe through which " Grace " flows into the Church, which derives from this its redemptive quality. But this interpretation is so depersonalised, so unrelated to God's other gifts and his work in the heart of the Christian fellowship, that it is in the end almost mechanical. It concentrates attention so exclusively on the Grace of God through the Eucharist as to forget that God is at work in the history of men and nations, and that what He does in men's hearts through Christ He wills to do throughout the whole world. Thus an entirely legitimate desire to stress the uniqueness of God's response to men in the community of the Holy Spirit may evacuate Christian devotion of its moral and spiritual content.

Clear thinking on this point is crucial to our whole understanding of Christian worship. Else we fall into one of two mistakes. Either we denude Christian worship of what is most distinctively Christian in it ; or we leave it so far in the air, isolated from everything else we know, as to make it appear almost irrelevant to the actual tasks of Christian men and women. The faith and worship of the Christian fellowship are the matrix of the distinctively Christian values and the Christian interpretation of life. And if we take the New Testament as our guide I do not think there is much room for doubt that the Christianisation of the world's life is meant to proceed from the centre outwards rather than inwards from the circumference.

But the aim of all Christian devotion is that men should become more responsive to the claims and gifts and tasks which God presents to them in the other aspects of their experience. Men are meant thereby to be redeemed from blindness, listlessness and selfconcern, and liberated into new insight and richer service for the glory of God. To whatever extent it does not result in this, worship is falling short of God's glory. Its truth and reality are tested, as Canon Quick finely observes, " not by any intensity of its own secluded devotion, but rather by its power to extend its meaning and influence beyond its own limited sphere, so as to give a Godward direction and interpretation to activities where God is no longer the object of the limited consciousness." [1]

Christian worship finds its fulfilment when men, through Christ, are admitted to communion with God's redemptive activity in the world. God is glorified when His sons " finish the work He has given them to do." Thus the worship of the Church fails if it does not succeed in relating the response of men to God's other claims in the broad field of life as a whole, and the wide, rich interests of humanism, with their specifically religious acceptance of His self-impartation through Christ.

The conclusion seems therefore to follow that these other and manifold forms of value—the claims, enrichments, interests and activities of the actual world in which our lives are spent—must be brought inside

[1] *The Ground of Faith and the Chaos of Thought*, pp. 135-136.

Christian worship. Not in the hope of making it attractive to a larger number of people by adding a topical interest to our Services, but for two, more profound, reasons. First, because they are part of God's work and integral to the cause of His Kingdom.   If God is the Creator of the world, then the establishment of His sovereignty—when His will is done on earth, as it is in heaven—cannot be confined to religious concerns. Secondly, because a right attitude to the so-called secular interests in life is part of what is meant by conversion ; and conversion is, for the Christian religion, the end for which worship is intended.

That religion means primarily worship is one of those truths that the clergy have learnt too well and the English layman has scarcely learnt at all. Hence that deplorable and disastrous breach (which seems to be widening rather than narrowing) between the point of view of the clergy and that of the people to whom they minister. The clergy tend to regard Christianity as chiefly a matter of devotional exercises, the laymen as chiefly a matter of Christian conduct. Hence they are apt to get at cross purposes. The people complain about the " clerical mind " and think that the parson is only interested in persuading them to attend services which have no obvious bearing on life. The parson breaks his heart by lamenting that some of the best Christians in his parish—better, perhaps, than those who frequent the Services—very seldom set foot inside the Church. On both sides there is misunderstanding. But, in fact, as Dr. Streeter would say, " both are right and both of them get prizes." Christianity *is* a way of living—which is what the pious sometimes forget ; but a way of living centred upon God—which is what the practical Christian must remember. Christianity, after all, is a religion : its centre of gravity is in the divine will : it is a life hid with Christ in God. The essence of Christian morality is " not to be conformed to this world." The very meaning of Christian discipleship is the consecration of man's life to God as He is made known to us in Christ. Therefore worship *must* come in the first place ; and the Church has been entirely right in the tremendous stress which it has laid upon it.

The danger of religiously-minded people is to think that devotional and liturgical exercises are all that the will of God for the world requires of them. But the primary emphasis in Christian worship is the acknowledgment of God's sovereignty : Our Father, hallowed be thy name. That means the submission of our thinking to the truth as it is in Christ Jesus, and the testing of our conduct and policies by God's will for men as Christ reveals it. Thus the very conception of worship implies the idea of lifelong conversion—a gradual re-direction of attitude. To worship in the full Christian sense entails a far-reaching revolution in the ways we think and the values we acknowledge. This truth is frequently forgotten, with the result that worship degenerates with fatal ease into sentimentalism. A man may be thoroughly conscientious, he may be genuinely sincere in his private religious devotion, and yet remain fundamentally un-Christian in the whole tenor and content of his thinking about the great affairs of the world, or about such matters as his investments, into which the spirit of worship has not yet penetrated. This is the danger of many congregations, and one reason why Christianity seems to achieve relatively little in the moralisation of the world's life. The right criticism about the Church is not that it puts the worship of God first—what else is it in the world for?—but that so many of us fail to realise how great is the demand made by worship if God indeed fulfils the law of Christ.

The authentic worship of the Christian Church must thus be always dynamic and transforming. We use glib phrases about "loving God," but what vast issues are not in fact contained in them! It involves the education of a lifetime, in the growing apprehension of truth, the training of our appreciation and our standards of excellence and beauty, the enrichment and deepening of our sympathies. To love God is not primarily a matter of stimulating religious emotions. That may do us a great deal of harm. If we are worshipping a false God—which means, for Christians, one less good than the God and Father of our Lord Jesus Christ—then the more intense our religion the less shall we be advancing in Christianity.

It is not, for example, a valid excuse for debilitating and sentimental hymns that " the people like them " because they are familiar and that, though they may not be good poctry—may be, indeed, quite shameless drivel—yet they help to evoke religious feelings. For if God is perfect Truth and perfect Beauty people *ought not* to like that kind of thing, and worship ought to be teaching them something better. Vigilantly we must " keep ourselves from idols." About everything connected with worship we must be constantly asking Is it true ? Is what it is trying to express worthy of the God whom Christ has revealed to us ? So that the very idea of loving God and worshipping Him " in spirit and reality " involves the idea of " being transformed by the renewing of our minds, so that we may prove what is the will of God "—in our moral, æsthetic and intellectual attitudes.

We are thinking, remember, about Christianity, not about un-particularised " religion." Religions are distinguished from one another not chiefly by differences of " externals," which are more or less constant in all religions, but by their ideas of the God they worship. The nature of Christianity imposes a certain definite character on its worship : its moral and intellectual content is peculiarly and decisively its own. Thus the Christian idea of worship must not be too lightly identified with other conceptions now widely popular. It must not, for example, be equated with that subjective meditation on the wonder and mystery of things which is prescribed by " scientific humanism." It is directed to a living God to whose will we are to be conformed. It is not sufficient to identify it, as is suggested by a distinguished biologist, with " that irrational, alogical element which is the most valuable contribution of religion to life."[1]

[1] J. Needham : *The Great Amphibium*, p. 78 ; *cf.* p. 5, " the essential component of religion is mystery and mystical experience." For a searching estimate of the social loss involved in the jettisoning of social worship, see the first and last chapter of *The Bleak Age* by the Hammonds.

" In the middle ages," writes Dr. Needham, " men made themselves eunuchs for the Kingdom of Heaven's sake, and in the future the same invitation will be extended to us to suppress our sense of the holy, to stamp it out and confront defiantly a world denuded of awe or mystery. Such a deicide will be a homicide too. . . . That is why it seems to me that it is now more necessary than ever to participate actively in religious rites, and to maintain firmly the fundamental validity of the religious experience as a characteristic activity of the human spirit. . . . There is no reason for denying that once this admission is made organised religion follows automatically." [1]

" In an age dominated by science " this protest is of real value. I do not wish to seem anything but grateful for it. Yet it is, I think, necessary to insist that this conception nevertheless falls short of worship as Christianity conceives it. For an " alogical core of the universe " is not the object of Christian faith and loyalty.

Indeed, this whole philosophy of the " Numinous " taken over, perhaps too lightheartedly, by some English thinkers from Germany, seems to be open to very grave objection. Some of our theologians have seized upon it as offering philosophical justification for traditional elements in the " catholic " cultus. But it is, surely, a dangerous alliance. No sane person is likely to suppose that the human reason can " define " God. A God defined is a God finished. True religion involves a sense of distance, and there is a danger lest, in our eagerness to relate worship to the common day, religion evaporate in familiarity. It is also true that the thrill and wonder of the " Grace and truth which came through Jesus Christ " presuppose the vast, stupendous depths of Divine being and reality

[1] *Op. cit.*, pp. 41–42.

which are incommunicable to man's experience and inapprehensible by finite spirits. Yet, unless there is real correspondence between the being of God and the mind of man, the Christian assumptions are false. Christians do not worship a vague *Numen*, but One whose character we know—the God and Father of our Lord Jesus Christ.

2. THE ART OF WORSHIP

But in saying this we have moved a step further and are viewing the question from a new angle. Christian worship is a means of grace but also an instrument of education. It is public worship more than anything else which moulds the theology of Christian people. Therefore one of the functions of worship is to provide a school of education in the Christian faith and way of living. Nobody will dispute the assertion that worship ought to be leading people to God. But this must mean that those who take part in it are thereby gathered within an active process of Christianisation in mind and temper and in their attitude to life as a whole. What is said and done must be an expression of that response to God and the world which is given to us through the Spirit of Christ. It should feel as if we believed in the Resurrection. It should be a potent instrument of evangelism. Even the stranger coming in casually should feel himself in the presence of something sincere, spontaneous, hopeful and constructive, which at once invites and constrains him to learn more of the

Source from which it issues. Where the group that
meets in the parish church is of low spiritual vitality,
it is worship that should nourish and stimulate it.
It should be evoking from congregations more than
they have yet learnt to offer. It should be the
growing point of the Christian community. It is
therefore of the utmost importance that worship
should not say or suggest anything unworthy of the
Christian religion.

For religious worship is an art, and indeed the
supreme art of Christendom, embracing all art-
forms within it. As such, it is seeking to *express* something through its own proper artistic medium.
There are thus two vital necessities. First, that what
it is seeking to express shall not be unworthy of the
God it worships ; secondly, that all its constituent
elements shall be made organic to its avowed purpose.
It ought to be possible after any Service to ask—
What was that Service saying ? and we ought to ask
about any Service—Does it really say what it means ?
Its medium is, to a very large extent, traditional and
stylised material : and we must not underrate the
value of traditional customary forms charged with
historical associations, even if imperfectly understood,
as the vehicle of unspoken convictions. Thereby the
congregation at worship is united with historic
Christian experience and with profound spiritual
forces which have moulded what is best in our
English heritage. Especially is this true of village
churches, where life is still largely ruled by tradition.

But the priest always needs the prophet. And these
forms need to be kept vital by the constant play of

experimental criticism.[1]   As an art worship must be
formal.   There is nothing in the least incompatible
between formal art and spontaneity.   Some of the most
perfectly spontaneous and lyrical creations of art have
worked through rigidly conventional forms.   This is
true not only in poetry and music, but also in painting,
sculpture and architecture.   It is therefore a quite
false ideal—as the Free Churches have begun to find
out[2]—to hope that by making worship informal we
should thereby make it more spontaneous.

But formal does not mean lifeless or mechanical.
And what is here past comprehension is how it has
ever been allowed to happen that Christian worship
should become dull.   It may be unskilled and badly
done—so are many exciting melodramas ; it may be
primitive in its artistic expression, thin and
impoverished in its religious content ; but how it
should be possible for anybody to allow what is done
in the name of Christ to appear dull, tedious and
uninteresting—that we must regard as inexplicable.
It can only be that clergy and people have not understood what it is they are trying to do.   They have
acquiesced in something that just happens instead of
making something worth while.

True, that on the whole English Churchgoers make
lamentably small demands on the clergy.   The
rector does what they call " taking the service,"
and that as a rule is all they expect of him.   They
may look for help and stimulus from his preaching,

[1] *Cf*. T. S. Eliot on " Tradition " and " Orthodoxy " in *After
Strange Gods*, p. 29.
[2] *Cf*. E. R. Micklem, *op. cit.*, p. 54.

as from his friendship and his pastoral care ; but
the Service is just something that happens. The
tragedy is that so many incumbents should be content to accept this position. There are men who
prepare their sermons elaborately yet give no thought
to the Service itself. Yet all the while it is preaching
the sermon for them, or else—as far more commonly
happens—cancelling out the effect of it in advance.
Suggestion is always stronger than logic. And the
fact is that in scores of churches in England we are
recklessly throwing away our chance simply through
lack of creative imagination in the planning and
ordering of our public worship.

It is not by any means only the fault of parsons.
Many of those who are working for something better
are defeated by reactionary parishioners. In some
parishes the bitter truth is that the people who most
frequent the church are the most fanatical obscurantists. If such as these are allowed to control policy
it is not much use having the young confirmed. The
parish church will not be a home for them. Yet
there is, just on the fringe, a very large number of
young men and women ready and even eager to be
drawn in, if our worship becomes less unimaginative.

Yet, however much may be hoped from effective
lay-cooperation, it is plain enough that the chief
responsibility must rest on the shoulders of the
clergy. After all, leadership in prayer and worship
is the primary task for which a man is ordained. It
is, I venture to say, the most important and responsible
of our ministerial functions and should be the first
claim on our mind and spirit. But what does not yet

seem to be fully realised is that this is a specialised job and as time goes on will become so increasingly. It calls not only for certain innate gifts, but for careful preparatory training and for assiduous exercise and discipline. It is as much a special vocation as that of the poet, architect or doctor, and demands, like these, technical equipment. Yet it is left almost entirely to chance. We do not ask much of theological colleges. Perhaps, as it is, the task that is set them is impossible. But it should not be unreasonable to ask that ordinands may at least be capable of reading aloud the Bible and Prayer Book in a natural voice, with some sense of rhythm and some appreciation of English prose. Perhaps, too, we might ask for some experience in preparing and leading informal devotions : far too many meetings are wrecked by the parson's prayers at the opening and the close. I do not suggest that this is enough : but a man who can do well what is prescribed for him will be able later, as he matures, to offer some contribution of his own.

This is needed mainly in two directions—in using the forms of Service we have, and in fashioning those that we need but have not yet. The Services in the existing Prayer Book need to be so worked upon and interpreted as to make them a sensitive medium to express the worship of twentieth-century Christians.

We have insisted above that Holy Communion is the true archetype of Christian worship. But it needs to be sustained and interpreted by other, non-sacramental, Services ; and in fact the Church has from the first taken over the Synagogue type of Service— the word-of-God Service, as the Germans call it—

consisting of prayer, Scripture and instruction as preface or support to the Liturgy. We must recognise that for most modern Englishmen " going to Church " implies this kind of Service—that is, in effect, Morning or Evening Prayer. Many clergy regard this as deplorable, but, welcome or unwelcome, this is the fact. Rightly or wrongly this is the form of worship with which most of our people are familiar ; and for very many it is their one contact with the teaching and worship of the Church. Therefore whatever " views " we may hold, an obligation rests on the parson to make the most that can be made of these Services, as a gateway through which the average Churchgoer may be led to the heart of Christian conviction.

It might seem to require a certain ingenuity to adapt the daily office of monks, as it emerged in 1552, as a Sunday Service for modern laymen. But a very great deal can be done, given only some judgment and imagination, without over-stepping the bounds of conformity. The Prayer Book provides the material : the minister's function is to interpret it.

We have to do the best that is possible with the forms provided in the existing Prayer Book. But I cannot fail to record my conviction that over and above the Prayer Book Services we need something more experimental to sustain, interpret and supplement them, if the Church is to answer the call of the new age. The Prayer Book superbly enshrines the genius of English-speaking Christianity : but it needs creative re-interpretation. The Prayer Book Services, by themselves alone, are inadequate, both in form and content, to the religious needs of the twentieth century. There are many public occasions in our time, which in 1662 were not contemplated. There are new approaches to life and religion, a revolutionised attitude to Scripture, a far greater conception of the Universe, a changed æsthetic and intellectual idiom, which combine to require new forms of expression as the vehicle of contemporary religion. We are faced with the task of re-interpreting the traditional legacy of Christian worship in the artistic idiom of a new age. This is a task far more demanding. It needs a rare combination of qualities : scholarship and experiment must meet together, restraint and imagination must kiss each other.

We cannot expect to produce to order the geniuses who will carry the work through for us. But it is surely the function of Bishops, as the chief priests and pastors of their dioceses, to encourage clergy and people in this task of liturgical experimentation. It is tragic that so many of them confine themselves to the attempt to secure standardisation and define the permissible limits of eccentricity. If in default of episcopal leadership the inferior clergy make bad mistakes or have given up trying to do anything, it cannot be said to be entirely our fault. Yet under the pressure of sheer necessity a great many attempts are being made. Some are mere unskilled improvisation, some are truly creative invention. The latter term may be fairly applied to some of the services in Liverpool Cathedral and to that used at the enthronement of the present Archbishop of Canterbury, as well as to some of the admirable suggestions which have been published by the B.B.C.[1] Thus there is gradually accumulating, in the cathedrals and larger parish churches, to say nothing of school and college chapels, a great deal of useful material, some of which at least deserves preservation. If anyone could devote skill and leisure to editing and publishing this material he would be making a big contribution to the revival of worship in England.[2]

Such a revival needs the cooperation of all sections and schools of thought in the Church. For the decline into which we have fallen, the Liberals and the Evangelicals are at least partly to blame. Disliking Anglo-Catholic ceremonial, they have allowed themselves to assume that the working alternative to High Mass is something flat, conventional and too lengthy. They have even accepted the dangerous heresy that " externals " in worship are unimportant, whereas in fact they are of enormous importance.

But we are passing now into a new era. Old fears and suspicions are dying out. Party cries and allegiances are becoming obsolete. We are learning to believe in the Church of England. Anglicanism has all the cards in its hand. It has its rich historical background, its tradition of intellectual freedom, its legacy of ordered experimentalism, its native gift for restrained magnificence and austere splendour in worship, and

[1] *Services for Broadcasting* (B.B.C., 1930).
[2] The book should be published with loose leaves, each Service or act of worship on a separate page, and each obtainable separately at a cheap rate, the leaves being stocked by the Publisher in large quantities. In this way the Services could be brought within reach of any parish church that desired to use them.

it has inherited the noblest language yet moulded by the lips of man. We have now to work trustingly together to embody this inheritance in new forms, open to all truth, but strong in our own, and so to rebuild the Church of the English people.

3. THE ORDERING OF WORSHIP

In conclusion, I venture to offer a few suggestions for the actual ordering of Services. It must be remembered that public worship cannot be, and should not attempt to be, like private devotion or an informal prayer-meeting transferred from the home to a Church building. Its aim and character are entirely different. It is a corporate and symbolic action. It is neither to be expected nor desired that every phrase and every part of the Service should be equally significant and appealing to every individual taking part. It is the worship of the Body corporate. It is meant to be a recapitulation and evocation of Christian experience, so fashioned that each individual can make his response to the total impression. It is bound to be " stylised " and universalised, and is best thought of as a kind of drama—only that here the " audience " are the " actors " and that the whole worshipping congregation ought to be caught up within the action.

The form of worship is universal, but it ought not therefore to be abstract. It is stylised, but not therefore lifeless. The importance of words, forms and ceremonials is primarily psychological. We can hardly suppose that one form of words or one order of ceremonial usage is more pleasing to God than another. One, of course, may suggest a true and another a false idea of God, and in so far they are matters of Christian principle. But, as between various possible ways of ordering and expressing our worship, assuming a fully Christian theology, it would seem that the primary consideration should be the extent to which they help or hinder the receptiveness of those taking part to God's renewing and redeeming Presence. And this is partly at least a matter of temperament, education and social tradition. Not all congregations need the same thing. If we could once get that clearly recognised it would be the end of much barren controversy. In any case it does not need arguing that leadership in worship requires at least some study and understanding of the principles of Group Psychology.

The minister's business is not to " preach " the Service, or to make it a means to *his* self-expression. He is there to lead the worshipping congregation. But it must depend largely on him whether or not the Service is an instrument for the creative expression of their worship. Of course it is true that liturgical forms of worship are meant, partly, to safeguard congregations against the vagaries of individual ministers. Yet even set forms need interpretation : stage directions presuppose actors : and even in the conduct of Matins and Evensong a great deal depends on the minister. It is his inalienable responsibility. The personal factor can only be eliminated by having recourse to a Tibetan prayer-wheel. No parson, however experienced, can devote too much thought or trouble to the way in which he orders these Services.

It is not merely the method of " taking " them—the control of voice, movement and so forth—but the planning of the Service itself which demands anxious thought and preparation. And, after all, we have fairly wide discretion. Even inside rubric and custom a great deal is left to ourselves. For example, the Book provides the words : but it says nothing which prescribes the *tempo*. And few things more defeat the spirit of worship than the breathless rush, at uniform pace, with which the Service is apt to speed its way from Dearly Beloved to the Blessing, with never a pause or a change of rhythm. Nor, as a rule, is nearly enough time allowed for the people to stand up and kneel down. Nothing in any rubric forbids the intercalation of silent periods, whether at the beginning or in the course of it.

So again we are told how to begin the Office ; there is nothing which makes it illegitimate to preface it with some introduction, whether of Scripture, music, or silence, which may help to create a receptive atmosphere. But this is of quite crucial importance. The opening words are vital to the whole Service. A dead, conventional opening is fatal. And one of the weakest points in the Anglican Service is the way in which it plunges at once, without preparation or preliminary, into the words of the General Confession. After all, the Lord's Prayer is the Christian model, and the order is presumably of importance. It is only after Hallowed be Thy name, Thy Kingdom come, Give us our daily bread, that the Master of prayer introduces the note of penitence.

But the preface provided for the Service in

the second Prayer Book of 1552 is not properly part of the office. In the 1928 book it is printed, as it should be, detached as an introduction to the office itself, which begins—O Lord open Thou our lips. We are not obliged to use this introduction, and it is, I should hold, necessary to devise other introductory forms. The easiest, simplest and probably best is, first, a period of silence prefaced by a few words of direction, and then one or two sentences of Scripture, freely and deliberately selected to strike the keynote of the whole service. When the General Confession is used it should be occasionally and with emphasis, as, for instance, on Sundays in Lent ; but even then the really right place for it is considerably later in the Service, as, for example, after the Sermon.

Once more, it is expressly provided in the revision of 1928 that the minister may pray in his own words " after the conclusion of Morning or Evening Prayer or of any service contained in this Book." This, surely, is not mere concession ; it is meant to suggest an ideal. The revisers do not want us to be content with reading collects out of a book ; they want us to lead the people in prayer.

The ideal which is there suggested can be interpreted in a great many ways. The true value of " extempore " prayer resides in its relevance, not in its unpreparedness. But in fact whatever we do or say, or allow to be said or done, in Church is leading—or misleading—the people. Every phrase, note, pause or gesture is conveying a true or a false suggestion about God and the Christian way of life. Therefore

K

we need to be " very jealous " for the honour and glory of the God we worship. We must exclude from our Churches at all costs the insincere, the slovenly and the trivial, and no smallest detail is unimportant— from the poise of the celebrant at the high altar to the cleanliness of the hassocks in the back pews.

Unity in conception and structure, the subordination of parts to one whole, are among the obvious qualities of good art. By contrast, what is often the worst failure in the worship of the Church as we know it, is its distracted, episodic character. Lessons, Psalms, Hymns, Prayers and Sermon seem too often at Matins or Evensong to have no intelligible inner relation, and to subserve no one controlling idea. So far as possible this must be counteracted. The Service should *move* from one point to another within the unity of an organic whole. It cannot do this if the first lesson is the bloodthirsty saga of Deborah, the second a series of healings on the Sabbath,[1] and the Sermon about something quite different. Ideally, the Service on every Sunday ought to have its own distinct " note," so that in the course of the Church-year the chief factors in Christian faith and life should find their due expression in worship.[2] At least the various elements in the Service must be organic to one leading idea. If this involves a departure from the Lectionary in selecting the passages of Scripture, that liberty was

[1] As is actually the case at Morning Prayer on the Second Sunday after Trinity in the revised lectionary.

[2] A tentative scheme of this kind was put forward in the " Proper " published in the so-called Grey Book ; suggestions for the hymns Sunday by Sunday at the end of *Songs of Praise* are based upon it,

approved in the Homilies, and may even be said to
have been urged upon the Clergy in the seventeenth
century. We should do well to claim it in our own
day.

The prayers that follow after the third collect are
now, by common consent, at discretion. It is therefore quite possible for ministers to provide that at
least Lessons, Prayers and Sermon should balance
and support one another. The Sermon, at any rate,
is in our own hands. There are, roughly speaking,
two kinds of Sermon. There is the full-length Sermon
or lecture discussing big questions of faith and conduct,
regarded as a whole in itself, independently of a
Service of worship, and followed by a prayer and the
blessing. This kind has, I believe, a great future.
It may be that the best arrangement is that the Sermon
should always be detachable from the Service of
worship preceding it, and that it should be made easy
for the people to be present at either or both.[1]

But there is also the more familiar kind which is
contained in a Service of worship. This presents
extraordinary difficulty both to the preacher and
to the congregation. But if we retain this kind
of preaching we can turn the necessity to glorious
gain by making it part of the whole act of worship.
Its general theme must be that of the whole Service.
Its treatment, of course, is the preacher's contribution ; vitality, freshness, independence and humour

---

[1] *E.g.*, a Sunday morning might be arranged thus—Morning
Prayer (half an hour)—Hymn—Sermon (half an hour)—Hymn
—Holy Communion. People could come for Matins only or
Sermon only or Holy Communion only, or for Matins and
Sermon, or Sermon and Holy Communion.

may supply not only the necessary relief but also enrichment to the complete whole. (The fool in Shakespeare will illustrate this point.) But it must lead naturally into prayer again, and should be followed by prayer from the pulpit. The proper end to a sermon, I suggest, is " Let us pray," not a peroration or the rather conventional " And now." It may well lead into a period of silence or meditation directed by the preacher, which should then be gathered up into spoken prayers which have been composed or provided beforehand. All this will obviously be much easier if the Sermon is placed in the middle of the Service, not at the end, as has become customary.

It ought, perhaps, to be said quite frankly that not every newly ordained man would be wise to attempt what is here suggested, or anyone to attempt it on every occasion. Everybody must use his own judgment. But in one way or another the Sermon and the rest of the Service must be held together.[1] And of this, in principle, I am certain, that in sitting down to prepare his sermon the first question that a man should ask himself is—Into what prayer is this going to lead the people ? He can then plan out both the Service and the Sermon. In Churches where there is more than one minister this entails close consultation between all concerned, including, of course, the organist. It should not be too much to

---

[1] I am thinking now about parish churches, where the clergy do most of the preaching themselves. The problem of visiting or " strange " preachers is one about which there are no known rules.

expect this : though too often it is quite obvious that none of them has given a moment's thought to it till the last minute in the vestry, and the ministrants are all at cross purposes.

The remaining element in the preparation is the choice of the hymns, and this needs laborious trouble. To choose them casually for a month in advance without reference to the rest of the Service or even the subject of the Sermon is to give up the attempt altogether. It may mean a whole morning's work to make the right choice for a given Sunday ; but to grudge whatever time may be needed is to waste all the rest of the time we spend on the preparation and ordering of the Service. Irrelevant hymns will kill everything else.

But nothing devised by perverse ingenuity can so successfully ruin an act of worship as the ceremony of " giving out notices." A string of remarks about whist-drives and jumble-sales intruded into an interval in the Service hopelessly shatters the atmosphere of worship. Notices should be ruthlessly cut out. If we cannot afford to print what is necessary, at least we can publish them at some other moment—before the Service or when it is over. The same applies to the Banns of marriage. If the Church Assembly is interested in worship it could make a most fruitful contribution to it by a Measure permitting banns to be published by being posted in the Church porch. Failing that, we must find another solution.

The question of music is far too contentious for a layman like myself to risk an opinion. Fortunately there is ample advice available. But one point is surely beyond argument—that we cannot tolerate in the worship of God a standard conspicuously inferior to that which all the potential worshippers can hear any evening at home on the wireless. Parish churches cannot afford not to keep up with a rapidly rising standard. The apology which is commonly offered is to emphasise the poverty of the resources which the average parish church can command. But most parish churches would be well advised to forget all about cathedral services, to use the natural voice most of the time, and to concentrate on congregational singing of really good, clean virile hymns, and a limited number of chants. Let me choose the hymns for my people, and let who will teach them their theology ! The selection of hymns is of crucial importance ; and without joining the battle of the hymn-books, I believe that the introduction of *Songs of Praise* will double a congregation in two months.[1]

[1] There is an excellent chapter on Music in Worship in Archdeacon Hunter's book *The Parson's Job*.

CHAPTER V

THE NEW CHRISTIAN MORALITY

1. TRADITION AND EXPERIMENT IN ETHICS

"IF the light that is within thee be darkness, how great is that darkness." But how can we be sure that it is not? That is the problem of this generation. No preacher who speaks about right and wrong as though all were agreed in the meaning of those words is addressing the audience in front of him. Just what *is* the right course of action in our tangled and complicated age? That is what they most want to know. Neither conscience nor social tradition seem to offer any secure criterion. All our certitudes have become "problems." We speak about the problem of the Family, the problem of Patriotism and so forth, finding ourselves tortured with misgivings in the sphere of the most direct moral duties. Perhaps for the first time in Christian history Christian parents find themselves at a loss how to instruct their children in conduct. So widespread is our moral insecurity. And the drift away from the Churches may perhaps be very largely explained by a resentful feeling of disappointment that they do not provide people with help at the point where they are most conscious of needing it. The conspicuous detachment from the Church of the young married couples of the professional classes seems here to be specially significant.

Admittedly without some moral tension any civilisation must stagnate. History is always in transition ; moral traditions are always in the making. The young are nearly always dissatisfied with the prevailing and established standards, and but for this fertilising criticism moral ideas would quickly become petrified into unexamined taboos. The discontent of the rising generation is the oxygen both of religion and morality. In periods of specially rapid change, when the bonds of society are being dissolved by new and little understood forces, whether spiritual or material, and new intellectual emancipations demand a revision of all the accepted axioms, the process is violently accelerated. At such times the younger people suspect that traditional standards are " mere conventions " imposed on society by its vested interests and bound up with the sterlising legacy of a now discredited religion. Thus criticism of religion, as Marx said, is the beginning of all criticism. The first result is the heady doctrine that " right " and " wrong " are merely relative terms which exist by " convention " and not by " nature " and have no real or metaphysical basis. This leads to the repudiation of all standards and a crude, fierce gospel of self-expression. This stage quickly brings disillusionment and passes into anxious enquiry for constructive principles of conduct. At such times both philosophy and religion are chiefly preoccupied with ethics, and the drama tends to become moral debate.

This cycle is more or less regularly recurrent. Many of the problems which are being canvassed in contemporary fiction and drama are raised, sometimes in almost identical form, in Euripides, Plato and Aristophanes. In the flowering time of the middle ages, at the Renaissance and at the Revolution, Europe passed through that same turmoil of ethical scepticism and confusion and attempted ethical reconstruction in which the whole world is involved today. It is steadying to bear this in mind. Our difficulties are not unique : the post-war mood is a commonplace of history, and the moral predicament in which we find ourselves has precedent enough in the human record.

Yet the predicament seems to be unprecedented both in the violence of its impact and in the world-wide range of its incidence. The moral bewilderment of our own time is at once more general and more radical than mankind as a whole has yet experienced. We have been subjected to the pressure of all possible forces of disintegration within the shortest time-span conceivable, and indeed within one normal lifetime. In many parts of the world today men whose fathers were naked savages are skilled engineers and technicians, and the sons of men whose lives were surrounded by uncriticised tribal custom or the dead moral dogmas of the Koran are now Bachelors in Arts and Science. This change is, I think, unexampled in the breathless rapidity of its tempo, and it may be allowed to stand as a symbol of the first three decades of the twentieth century. It is not to be wondered at if the pace and suddenness of these readjustments are putting a heavy strain on the heart.

The volcanic upheaval of the war, overwhelming us in bitterness and anxiety to the third and fourth generation, broke on a world already becoming exiled from nearly all its accustomed securities. The critical solvents of the new knowledge were already at work on established loyalties. The westernisation of the backward peoples was already destroying the old tribal faiths and uprooting nations from their ancestral allegiances. Technical and economic development was changing the pattern of western society, revolutionising the social order, shifting the centres of political force and causing ominous cracks in that structure of capitalism buttressed by democracy which had so magnificently enshrined the Queen. During the reaction under Edward VII[1] people were beginning to ask, Why shouldn't I ? Religion, at least as taught by the Churches, was losing its hold on the professional classes—though the mild scepticisms of that period are the Sunday School lessons of today. (When we remember what was regarded up to the war as dangerous modernism we stand aghast at the thought of the obscurantism which we then mistook for enlightenment.) Questionings about creed and conduct were already widespread and unsettling : everybody was reading Bernard Shaw : Mr. Potter

[1] But the Edwardian emancipation was curiously superficial and hardly went deeper below the surface than Grundyisms and respectabilities. *Cf.* the remarks of Maurois about Edwardian drama and the censorship in *King Edward and his Times*, pp. 237–238.

repeatedly " losing his faith." Yet, despite the discordant voice of Nietzsche, liberal humanitarian ideals were still almost everywhere taken for granted, and whatever the doubts about Christianity, most Englishmen comfortably assumed that the main principles of the Christian ethic offered mankind permanent moral guidance.

The war not only brought to a crisis the latent poisons of disintegration : it annihilated all the remaining certainties. As the carnage dragged on its course, in which it became increasingly impossible to find any trace of moral justification, loyalties were wounded and smashed to death. When at length the blizzard came to an end, all the familiar landmarks had perished. The young emerged lost and uprooted from the moral certitudes of their predecessors, and with a consuming indignation against all those moral assumptions which seemed, not only to have failed, but to have so disastrously betrayed them. Everything that was " pre-war " was suspect. The young had no history at their backs. They seemed to themselves adrift in a world which began only after the Armistice, with no appeal to inherited experience and no principles that would stand the test.[1] The world had to be rebuilt from the ground, but they knew no foundation on which to build.

Meanwhile their disgust and disillusionment with the " Christian " and pre-war morality was completed by

[1] The effect of the experience on a young man and a young woman respectively has been described by Hugh Fausset in *Prelude to Life*, and Vera Brittain in *The Testament of Youth*. For an interesting study of its impact on the young in Germany, see Otto Piper's *Recent Developments in German Protestantism*.

the shame of the peace treaties. No wonder that they
were driven desperate and abandoned themselves to
the cult of a " good time "—for what else did life seem
to offer ? No wonder if they embraced the assump-
tion that all men and women over forty were not only
blind but insincere, and that all religious and moral
traditions were in themselves necessarily false. All
standards alike seemed to have broken down.

The wild epicurean reactions of the nineteen
twenties have now spent their force. They have been
succeeded by a profound seriousness. It is not, I think,
at all true to say that the young men and women of
the nineteen thirties are more morally lax than their
parents—such a judgment wholly misrepresents them.
They are, indeed, in a number of ways more stringent,
and many of them are shocked by the levity of their
senior post-war contemporaries. They are devoting
themselves with keen minds and uncompromising
sincerity to the task of understanding their world and
reconstructing its institutions. To describe the outlook
of this generation as a " revolt against Christian
morality " is a tragic misdirection of justice. It is a
search for a new morality, seeking for guidance wherever it may be found, and ready to welcome Christian
solutions if they can show cause why they should be
accepted. They will not be accepted on authority.
For what is most of all characteristic about the contemporary moral outlook is its thorough-going experimentalism. This is what makes the " new morality "
new. It is not an alternative to the Christian ethic
—nothing so systematic as that. Still less, as ruri-
decanal conferences are rather absurdly prone to

suggest, is it a recrudescence of paganism and a justification of sexual self-indulgence. (What demon put it into the heads of Christians that morality is all about sex ?) It is an experimental morality by contrast with a morality of tradition.

It is otherwise, no doubt, among other peoples. Driven by poverty and humiliation to a depth of desperation and bitterness that we can only with difficulty imagine, the young generation in Central Europe, and in those vast areas of the world in which Soviet rule is established, have surrendered themselves to a moral creed which must be regarded as antithetical to the ethic which rests on Christianity. Of that we shall have more to say later. But among ourselves the whole situation is still open and can still be redeemed. A generation that faces moral perplexity with such frank and open-eyed realism, such courage and such hatred of subterfuge, cannot be far from the Kingdom of God. In perfect good faith it may say and do things which make older people's hair stand on end : but the light within it is not darkness. It may be that if, during those years with which we are concerned in this estimate, I had not been allowed the double privilege of being a Fellow of an Oxford College and Vicar of a University Church, I might incline to a less hopeful verdict. But a man must write out of his own experience. And, in my view, the young men and women who are now passing from school and college into our ambiguous and distracted world are so fundamentally sound in quality and so essentially honest in outlook that they may be found to have " come to the Kingdom "

precisely " for such a time as this." They are determined not to be over-ridden by any appeal of sentiment or emotion, and are too hard-boiled to respect a
vague uplift. They are looking questioningly towards
Christ, who alone remains still undiscredited. The
whole future turns on the question whether the
Church has insight and courage enough to offer
them a convincing Christian leadership and to help
them to fashion in the new age a new and creative
Christian morality.

If the " new " morality is un-Christian—and some
of its experiments and suggestions do cut across
Christian principle—that is not merely because it is
new. Christianity is in itself a new morality. It was
thus that it first appeared in the world, transvaluing
the accepted values, undermining many established
traditions, and beginning to reconstruct the social
order from a new centre and on new foundations. It
first appeared as a dangerous revolution. It is
probable that the name Christian excited as much
terror and antagonism in the breasts of conservatively
minded Romans as the mention of " Reds " in a
West-end club today. It was a new moral dynamic
which expressed itself in changed ways of living. When
" the law " and the old codes had failed, both through
lack of inherent vitality and because their actual
prescriptions could no longer claim correspondence
with the patterns of a transitional society, Christianity
introduced a creative ferment which at once broke
down the decaying tissues and began to build a new
living system. At all its vigorous and inspired periods
it has proved this same regenerative power. Where

men have been in life-giving touch with the Spirit of the living Christ the Christian religion has always manifested this transforming ethical creativity. The song of the Church is always a new song : where men are " in Christ " there is " a new creation."

Thus the claim to be a new morality, at all times and in all places, pertains to the very nature of our religion. Its hold on the allegiance of the modern age will depend on its power to vindicate that claim, to embody its perennial inspirations in such new forms and patterns of conduct as the changed needs and conditions of life demand, and to fashion the recalcitrant materials of an unforeseen social evolution into a spiritual world-order. It is not the stuff out of which it is composed that makes a thing material or spiritual, but the purpose by which it is directed.

Christianity is a life, not a formula. The Christian ethic (as I have written elsewhere) is " not so much a code to be defended as an insight to be achieved " ; else it is merely the fossilised record of a long obsolete moral system which cannot maintain itself in a strange environment. The actual content of Christian duty must change with the changing generations. Not, of course, that the Christian way of living can ever be " shaped to the pattern of the world " in which at a given moment it dwells. Faiths and standards, like men and women, are only too easily shaped and moulded by the pressure of external circumstances. Life consists not merely in adaptation to environment but in mastery over it. And an ethic which is merely conformed to the outward conditions of a culture, and those thought-forms and behaviour-patterns which they impose on the bodies and souls of men, is but an echo of life, not a guide to it. This is specially true of the Christian ethic, which rests on an estimate of human activity irreconcilable with those assumptions with which the minds of twentieth-century men are being almost compulsorily indoctrinated. It cannot compromise its conviction that the centre of gravity for man's life is not to be found in this world at all. If Jesus was wrong at the centre of His thinking, then the Christian ethic is a false ethic. But if He was right, the conclusion follows that we cannot take bits of our Lord's moral teaching and " apply " them in a civilisation which rests on totally different assumptions. Our civilisation must " repent " before it can talk of " applying " Christianity. To be saved without being converted, which is what the contemporary world is asking for, is in the nature of Christian things impossible.

From this point of view the Christian ethic cannot conceivably be brought up to date. It can never be completely acclimatised in any form of secular civilisation, and must always stand as a witness and a protest against a too facile conformity to the ruling tendencies of a given period. Its citizenship is in heaven. Yet an ethic becomes merely formal, and to that extent morally sterilising, unless it is realistically related to the actual circumstances and conditions within which life must be lived, and the concrete problems of conduct about which decisions have to be made. These are in constant process of change. An ethic presented in terms of " rules " will and always must be anachronistic as a positive guide to right living. It will always reflect the conditions of the period in which it was formulated rather than those of contemporary life. Thus it can only escape from obscurantism at the price of avoiding all actuality.

In that period of solid confidence which was finally shattered by the war, the main principles of the Christian life were run into the moulds of a code which was perhaps generally sufficient in relation to those temporary circumstances. But those circumstances no longer hold. Scientific and technical developments, far-reaching economic changes, the emergence of a new range of problems as regards our duty both to posterity and to international cooperation, above all the spread of education and the dangerous enlightenment of new knowledge, have altered the whole pattern of moral action and complicated all moral choices. The accepted code has accordingly broken down.

Moreover, we have begun to recognise how deeply that code itself was coloured with the prevailing assumptions of its context. We are sceptical about its legitimacy, and refuse to equate " Christian morality " with the average moral standards of a past age, however much tinged with Christian emotion. And again, going back behind that, we suspect that all manner of alien elements have seeped into the Christian moral tradition and to some extent polluted the reservoirs. We may instance the Roman law of property, and definitely sub-Christian theorics about the authority of the sovereign state, which had almost come to claim Christian sanction. Nor can we forget that the " Christian " sexual ethic has been

L

promulgated exclusively by males, and predominantly at that by monks and celibates. We are not prepared to accept their prescriptions as permanent or as finally authoritative for the Christian conscience in the twentieth century.

Once more, contemporary thought is saturated with evolutionist presuppositions. To our way of thinking, life means movement. The idea of a faith once and for all delivered, whether in religion or ethics, cuts across all our approaches. The result is that an ethic of authority, contained in a code or a written text claiming universal applicability, is to us almost a contradiction in terms.

But the Christian ethic is not of this kind. The claim which the Church makes for the " finality " of the way of living revealed in Christ does not rest on authoritative texts. It does not extend to documents or prescriptions, whether of the Fathers or Councils, or even of the New Testament itself. It is not a teaching, but a Person, whom it calls the Way, the Truth and the Life. It is the eternal and final quality of " the mind that was in Christ Jesus," His sovereign insight and dedication, His supreme revelation and embodiment of the meaning of goodness itself within the conditions imposed upon Him by history. It is, yet more, His ever-renewed power to redeem and re-create human lives and to reproduce the fruit of His own spirit in all peoples and all generations, amid circumstances and demands completely unlike His own, which designates Him Lord of the moral universe. We do not know whither He is going ; we do not know the full and completed meaning of the Christian life in the world ; only that He is the way and the truth.[1] The actual content of the Christian ethic must be in continual change and development as life itself sets us new lessons and confronts us with fresh opportunities. The task of this Christian generation is to discover what *is* the Christian ethic in relation to our own time and place. In this the candour and objectivity of the seekers after a " new morality " should prove an invaluable reinforcement.

The demand for an experimental, as opposed to an authoritarian ethic, need not be at all inconsistent with acknowledging Christ's spiritual sovereignty. There is not, indeed, any real doubt that as between these two conceptions our Lord Himself is on the side of the moderns. It was for this that He challenged the antagonism of the most powerful interests in Palestine ; the stand that He made about the Sabbath was the initial cause of the Crucifixion. But He stood for freedom against formalism, not because He believed in evolution or in the relativity of history or in any other of our high-sounding theories, but because He believed in a living God, creative of Beauty, Love and Righteousness. And unless it is founded on that conviction, all our big language about freedom becomes a mere petition in moral bankruptcy.

But the ethical dynamic of Christianity is precisely that victorious conviction. " He that sitteth upon the Throne saith, Behold I make all things new." It is the faith of the Incarnation that God is ever

1 John xiv. 5, 6.

redeeming to Himself the manifold elements in the world's life, to incorporate them into the Body of Christ. The more vigorous its Christianity the less, therefore, will the Church be daunted by the magnitude of the ethical tasks before us. It will see in the new conditions and complexities with which in our time we are confronted, not more obstacles to Christian living, but fresh material for its achievement.

2. SOME ETHICAL TASKS OF THE CHURCH

Someone has said that predicting the future is " the most gratuitous form of error." It would be waste of time and ingenuity were we to attempt to forecast the system, whether social, economic or political, in which the society of the future is likely to organise its common life. The important questions about it are moral. Will mechanisation overwhelm spirit, or will spirit assert control over mechanism ? What will be its standards of valuation —will persons still be the slaves of things, as they are in the existing social order, or will it care supremely for persons and for things only so far as they serve the ends of personal and spiritual development ? Will it be self-centred and self-sufficient—an organised system of relations which holds good only within that society but without regard to the meaning of life itself ? Or will it be a city that hath foundations, in which the corporate life of men and women is redeemed, directed and sustained by communion with spiritual reality ? These are the primary Christian concerns ; and these are not vain speculations ; they involve instant and practical decisions. Has the Church the faith, insight and power so to recreate society from within that, whatever the shape of the new order, it will be a moral society of persons, not a mere complex of processes ? Are we to make history or to suffer it ? These are the questions which life today is asking us.

The Church cannot meet this situation with a merely traditionalist morality or with an attitude of condemnation. It is unfortunate that so many statements of Church opinion on living moral issues are negative and condemnatory in form, and give the impression that the Christian conscience has learnt nothing and forgotten nothing. " This conference deplores . . ." ; it is an old formula, but not the utterance of a living faith. We must not identify Christ's way of life with the social conventions of our predecessors. Can it really be doubted that through the ministry of scientific discovery and invention, the new psychological techniques and the opening of new possibilities in the elimination of chance and the conscious control of behaviour, God is not only setting us new problems but offering us fresh opportunities for victorious and creative Christian living ? Nor, I think, is it possible to deny that some of the new demands which are being made by the conscience of the twentieth-century man are true, in principle, to the mind of Christ.

The moral question which comes home most closely to contemporary men and women concerns the relationship between the sexes. It is not necessarily the most important, but it comes first in order of experience. And here we are moving into a changed climate. At present our course is erratic and unsteady through shoals of ignorance and reefs of crudity. But the new ideals of those relationships which are beginning to show on the horizon may yet be found to be more fully Christian than those which were assumed by our predecessors. The new demands which are making themselves heard are not due merely to lust and selfishness. And the Church will forfeit all its moral authority unless it has the courage to come to terms with the actualities of family life in the circumstances of our time. An apologetic and evasive attitude rules it out of court altogether. It must offer liberal, understanding and genuinely constructive moral guidance, not least in regard to those urgent questions bound up with the limitation of the family which are the points at which ethical perplexity presses most heavily on the modern conscience. We cannot hope to sanctify marriage by identifying the Christian interest with legislation which has become intolerable. Christianity has its own scale of values, and it cannot be God's will to sacrifice the possibilities of family life to the mere demands of respectability.

While I was in Australia last winter (summer) the Eucharistic Congress in Melbourne was made the occasion by the Roman Hierarchy for a vigorous output of propaganda — in its most indefensible form—against limitation of the family. The other Churches said nothing at all, leaving it to be inferred by the onlooker that they do not dissent from this deplorable teaching, and thereby deepening the alienation of morally sensitive people from their fellowships.

The considered Anglican judgment is on record in the report of the last Lambeth Conference ; but this document is not met with frequently on the bookstalls of the Australian railway stations.

It is more serious that in our own Church so many accredited teachers have ignored that judgment and some have tried to bring it into contempt. There are signs that a concerted attempt will be made to bring pressure on the next Conference to secure the reversal of that courageous statement. It is not in the least likely that the Bishops will be influenced by this agitation. But it does seem necessary to insist that any successful move in this direction would stultify that moral leadership which the Anglican Church is increasingly assuming, and deprive it of all right to offer guidance to the conscience even of its own members.

There is no slick answer to this perplexing problem ; and in each country it takes a different colour. Unemployment, economic stringency and a far more sensitive recognition of the rights both of wives and children are probably constant factors in all countries. But there are situations, as in Australia, where the short-term necessities of these factors appear to clash with the long-term necessity for a large increase in population. No one answer is universally right. But a merely negative answer must be false. If we compel sincere men and women to import shame, evasion and subterfuge into their most intimate relationships, how can we hope to Christianise home life, or to construct a Christian social order from its foundations in the home upwards ?

But phrases about a " Christian social order " may become dangerously misleading. There is no complete Christian programme for the re-constitution of society. In the nature of the case there can never be one. The spirit of Christ offers no direction in respect of detailed conduct or policy in the circumstances of the twentieth century. What it offers is a judgment redeemed and a will consecrated to the Father and access to regenerative resources which can resist the wearing down pressure of moral inertia and disappointment. It offers men vision and it confers fidelity. The task of the Church is not to put forward an alternative to the schemes of statesmen as they try to find their way to a better order, but to inspire them to produce their own and to supply that spiritual dynamic which can bring those schemes to victorious fulfilment. And it may be claimed that Christian public opinion has contributed with signal effectiveness to the new forward policy in Housing accepted at long last by the National Government.

But the technical factors which are involved, whether in politics or economics, are not part of the Christian revelation. Many Christians are good economists, and not all the fools are inside the Churches. But the Church possesses no revealed knowledge of governmental or economic techniques. It would be an irreparable mistake to identify the Christian solution with any particular programme put forward. A particular social credit scheme is not in itself more Christian than any other method that may prove workable. Nor, I think, is it possible to assert that a specially Christian sanctity inheres in the British system of Parliamentary government.   There may be under other conditions other effective instruments of freedom.   However much conscience may be affronted by the methods of contemporary Dictatorship, the " leadership " principle need not in itself be inconsistent with the Christian genius.   The task of the Church is to affirm that the State is the instrument of personality, not the end for which persons exist, and to inspire the labours and sacrifices of men and women of goodwill not merely to mitigate the existing system, but experimentally to construct another and less imperfect instrument of God's purpose.

Nevertheless, in any existing systems and in any alternatives that may be proposed, there are involved spiritual values on which the Church is bound to pronounce judgment.   And in a transitional age such as ours when values are confused and uncertain, it is not its least important prerogative to supply the world with a spiritual criterion.   For it is not seriously disputable that a new form of social organisation is even now taking shape, or that its pattern will differ very greatly from that which has been familiar to ourselves.   British civilisation in the last century sought to combine democracy in politics with individualistic capitalism in industrial and financial enterprise.   The experience of the post-war period has shown that the two are incompatible.   Either democracy must be sacrificed—as has happened almost everywhere on the continent—or capitalism must be superseded.

Capitalism as at present organised has broken down in the sphere of economics, and it has poisoned and corrupted politics. It has failed to deliver or distribute the goods, and the feverish efforts of the last decade to keep alive the capitalistic system have intensified its dangers in politics, but without redeeming its economic failure. In an age when the resources of production could secure an abundant standard of life to the whole of the world's population, millions are living below the poverty line, and vast numbers are actually starving. Capitalism can only maintain itself by condemning millions to unemployment with all its bitterness and humiliation. The moral indictment of the existing system is not more scathing or more obvious than its own economic incompetence to meet the necessities of a changing world.

There are probably very few thinkers who believe that capitalism *in its present form* can support the civilisation of the future. The attempts that are being made to adjust it to contemporary historical conditions are even more morally disastrous. Fascism is the next stage ahead of it. The inevitable trend of the process is towards a capitalism of monopoly organised on a nationalistic basis, which means in effect economic imperialism, as ruthless and as unscrupulous as warfare. There is little to distinguish its methods from the actual use of blockade in time of war, except that in this case all the belligerents—which means all nations without exception and even within the British Empire—are engaged in blockading one another. It is making a battlefield of two hemispheres. It is heading straight for unparalleled catastrophe. Yet we need not be

Marxians to recognise that this exceedingly dangerous new development is not caused by malignant wills : it is involved in the nature of capitalism and follows from its inherent necessities. But this means that the capitalistic system, at least in the forms in which it exists at present, is incongruous with both the moral and the economic realities of the new age.

The fundamental Christian objection to the existing capitalistic system, and to the banker's control of money from which it seems inseparable in England, is that it holds persons in helotry to the exigencies of financial policy. But money was made for man, not man for money. To say that the social services must be starved and sons and daughters of God kept in penury—at a time when poverty is the one evil which we have power to eliminate completely—because of the claims of a monetary policy is merely to say that the policy is a failure. If a system cannot be made to work on any terms tolerable to conscience nor without sacrificing men and women to an impersonal and abstract dogma, then it is the system that must be changed, not men and women that must be starved.

The Church has too long given the impression that it stands for the maintenance of the existing system. This has done Christianity grievous harm. We must not identify the Christian ethic with a system against which the awakened conscience ought to keep alive an effective protest. The presuppositions of western society are the contradictory of the Christian axioms ; for they value things more highly than persons, and make traffic in the souls of men. A social order resting on such assumptions can never be ratified by the Christian conscience.

Confronting it now as its one effective rival stands the stupendous experiment of Communism. The intense conviction, the will to sacrifice and the contagious missionary fervour which inspire and sustain that terrific movement, may well put Christianity to shame. It is fatally easy to represent Communism as the antithesis of Christianity. But the fact that it persecutes religion, represented to it by a decadent Church subservient to the privileged classes, must not be allowed to blind Christian judgment to the spiritual splendours inherent in it. We may regard its philosophy as false and abhor the cruel violence of its methods ; but the so-called crusade against its " atheism " is too much complicated by political motives for Christians to be advised to take part in it.

Soviet rule is the contradictory of British political traditions, and the popular instinct is not far wrong in regarding it as their most dangerous enemy. If we believe that the British tradition preserves elements of the highest importance for the moral development of mankind, it becomes our duty to safeguard it. But we do not safeguard our own tradition by condonation of its moral defects. Still less dare we equate it, in its present form, with the Christian ideal of the social order.

There is more truth in the Marxian dialectic than Christian apologists willingly admit. It is, for example, obviously true that the outward organisation of society, and predominantly its economic pressures, do condition men's moral attitudes, and for good and for evil have their effect on character. It cannot be doubted that our form of society does induce in its more fortunate classes too great a readiness to accept privilege as though it were inherent in the moral order. We do not really believe in our hearts that everybody is to count for one and nobody for more than one ; we do not love our neighbours as ourselves. And it is true of society as we know it that there is a real clash of class-interest between those who have and those who have not. That Marx's predictions have not worked out precisely in the form he anticipated, that their arbitrary and dogmatic assumptions can be easily exposed and refuted, does not affect the importance of this criticism. It is not effectively answered by ignoring it.

No religion which preaches salvation by the regeneration of the inward man, but glibly ignores those external circumstances which in any event condition character and may frustrate spiritual development, can expect its promises to be taken seriously. A passion for a radical reconstruction in the material bases of life is not in itself in the least " materialistic." It is that only if material well-being is regarded as the supreme value ; and it may be that this false valuation is the lie in the soul of bourgeois societies.

The answer of Christianity to Communism must be passionate, positive and constructive and express a will to no lesser sacrifices than those which inspire the Communist crusaders. *We are changing the world*, chant thousands of boys and girls in unison as they parade round Lenin's mausoleum. It is precisely what Christians mean, or should mean, when they gather round the altars of their Lord and say *We believe in God the Father*. They mean " This is God's world, and it is His will to make it a home wherein His sons and daughters can come to the fulfilment of themselves as persons made for communion with Him. He wills that we should take the material and mould it to the ends of spirit, fashioning it as the instrument of His purpose. Our lives are pledged that His will may be done on earth as it is in heaven."

The fundamental Christian objection to the Communist programme for society is that it is not genuinely Communism. No doubt it is true that all revolutions, whether æsthetic, moral or political, are determined by that against which they revolt and must take the forms imposed on them by the systems which they propose to supersede. Some of the worst features of Communism are thus in fact due to the sins of Tsardom. But although this should mitigate sentence, it does not and must not affect the moral verdict of the Christian conscience on its professed ideals. Communism, in its only true sense—*i.e.*, a community of persons with all those spiritual capacities which inhere in the nature of personality—is what Christians call the Kingdom of God. Communism, in the Soviet sense, despite those Biblical and Messianic elements which Berdyaef has disclosed in its ancestry, is almost what St. John calls " the world," a system which " lieth in the power of the evil." Since it is not genuinely communistic but the avowed dictatorship of one class, its loyalties subsist on antagonisms. Moreover, it confessedly regards persons merely as means to its own policies or as so much grist for its mechanisms, and esteems only those qualities which can be made subservient to its own ends. Thus it mutilates personality and, by equating the good for man with the triumph of its own system, Communism tends to falsify all values.

These are but different ways of describing the intrinsic evil of the Soviet polity, that it is a system of social relations wholly self-sufficient and self-centred—which is what the New Testament means by " the world." Self-centredness is the essence of sin and the root of all social wrong. Despite all its egalitarian language, Communism thus proves in practice to be the antithesis of community ; for community can never be realised till the principle of social cohesion is the conscious unity of societies in the Universal Spirit called God.

Communism, however, is not alone in this condemnation. All the societies of the modern world, whatever particular basis they adopt for their economic and political structures, are vitiated by the same principle. It needs of course to be fully recognised that no human society is entirely secular. No association of men and women on however humble a level but is, in its own degree, a manifestation of that " love " which has its ground in the Being of God. There is no society wholly apart from God " from whom all Fatherhood is named." Every kind of social organisation, from the most rudimentary to the most developed, has its essential bond of cohesion in the sharing of a common purpose which organises the Group yet transcends it, immanent in it, but yet not its product. It lives by partaking in a spirit. And so far as concerns the psychological process, the emergence of the Christian

Church may be rightly described in these terms. It can be truly said of any society that it is both from heaven and of men. However imperfect, sterile or perverted, yet that which has called it into being is at least some recognition of value (even if only honour among thieves), some response to spiritual environment, some sensitiveness to the Divine Spirit. Even the most worldly society has in it some spark of other-worldliness, which at best vitalises and ennobles, and at worst redeems it from total ignominy.

But there is no secular society which realises the full meaning of a true personal community. They all achieve a certain degree of harmony, but it is harmony at too low a level, which attains to a social solidarity at the price of ignoring or overriding large fields of personal value and concern. Or they so far restrict the area of community to their own self-contained group as to become in the long run a menace to it. To a certain point they go but no further. Their conscious goal is wholly within this world. Their aim is not consciously directed to the realisation of that true community, through a common partaking in the Divine Spirit, apart from which man's life remains frustrated.

This is the crux of the present situation. For the fact is that the world is now passing, through extreme difficulty and dislocation, from the separatisms and departmentalisms of the post-Reformation and post-Renaissance era, to some new and more comprehensive integration. It is groping its way towards a new synthesis of unity with individuality. And at present the passage is arrested by the decay of spiritual conviction. It seems as though men must choose between a chaotic and sterile individualism and a closely knit but self-centred group—by whatever name they may describe it—which constitutes a focus of unity but clashes both with other self-contained groups and the individuality of its own members.

The ferocious Nationalisms of our own time are in part, as we have already observed, the resultants of economic necessity, and in their turn help to exaggerate the false trends in the economic system. But they may be regarded quite justifiably as an attempted spiritual protest—mistaken but none the less to be held in respect—against that spurious post-war internationalism, concerned only with economic relationships, which ruthlessly disregarded all values, whether cultural, political or religious, not strictly relevant to its own interests. It was over-riding all local differences, tending to make the whole world Chicago. It was cynically contemptuous of all loyalties other than those of investments and dividends ; and indeed its most ignominious exhibition is the armaments combines across those frontiers which it is their ostensible business to defend.

The neurotic nationalistic movements are, in part, a reaction against this, and as such may claim some true positive value. For all the most vital contributions to the spiritual wealth of mankind come out of the life of a concrete society, with its own native history and tradition and its roots struck deep into a local soil. A cosmopolitan culture is no culture. The great artists and the great saints who belong to all times and to all peoples are themselves true children

M

of their own. Shakespeare and Goethe, St. Francis
and St. Augustine, all of them belong to the ages,
but none of them is in the least cosmopolitan. They
could have sprung from no other culture than that
which in fact both bred and inspired them. So again
" citizens of the world " are too often in very serious
danger of becoming citizens of no city and evading
those obligations to a living social tradition which are
two-thirds of the content of the good life.

The current reaction against internationalism is
thus not without some justification. Yet it is in its
present form disastrous. So long as each national
community is organised round itself as centre, tension
and finally conflict are inevitable. There is not,
indeed, any necessary conflict between the self-
fulfilment of local groups and their harmony in an
embracing whole. But the reconciliation is only
possible if the centre both of the groups and of the
whole is conscious submission to the Universal. Only
as men are reconciled to God are they reconciled to
one another. It must of course be thankfully recognised that beneath all its fears and antagonisms the
world of today is slowly learning its lesson. Under
the pressure even of sheer self-interest there is gradually
taking place a continual widening of circumference
in the area of acknowledged obligations. Even if our
practice belies it, we know that no man lives to himself.
And Christians should be eagerly in the forefront of
all movements in thought and policy towards more
effective integration and conspicuous in support of the
League of Nations. But even a world-state which was
organised on a principle of enlightened self-interest

would not yet be in accord with the Divine Purpose. The Brotherhood which the Gospel proclaims is the expression of the Divine Fatherhood. Therefore only a radical conversion can offer a radical and creative remedy for the ills of contemporary civilisation.

This, however, does not mean that the Christian need wholly despise self-regarding motives. If the world is ordered by Divine Providence, then the real interest of one must coincide with the welfare of all. But the more the Christian schools himself and others to appreciate what are the true interests which invest man's life with its worth and dignity, the more will he help to redeem earthly citizenships from their disharmonies and their frustration into the freedoms of Life Eternal. Precisely by what policies and what methods Community is most likely to be secured, Christianity does not in itself declare. Each Christian must act and vote as his conscience judges—assuming that he has done the best possible to keep that conscience sensitive and enlightened. His one inescapable obligation is, by training himself in the vision of God, to bring to all the decisions of his citizenship a judgment redeemed by the mind of Christ and a fixed resolve to refer all policies not to immediate national self-interest, but to the Plan of the Divine Kingdom— which includes the true welfare of his own people.

This obligation seems to involve a decisive repudiation of the claim to absolute sovereignty by the Nation State. So long as each nation remains a law to itself and the ultimate court of its own appeal, no people can realise its vocation as the servant of God's kingdom in history. Here the Christian is bound to take a stand, refusing to burn incense to Cæsar. It is also a part of the Christian's duty to take and to seek out opportunities of fostering personal relationships across political and economic frontiers, both within the nations and between them. And it goes without saying that the more vitally the Church revives as a fellowship in Christ, the richer will be the Christian contribution.

The decisive concern of the Christian ethic is in this matter of personal relationships. What we mean by "making civilisation moral" is making it serve the ends of persons. The machinery of any economic system is inevitably mechanical and impersonal. But so also is that of the human body. The chemical and physiological functions react according to their own principles. What makes a human life spiritual is the control of these organic processes by the conscious aims of personality. So an economic system would become spiritual if it were so controlled by the aims of spirit as to make it the instrument of persons and a means to enrich personal relationships. Notoriously at the present time our system thwarts and impedes this fulfilment, so that persons are the slaves of its mechanisms.

The appalling by-product of Unemployment is the worst example of this result. But just at this point, by a heaven-sent paradox, is a fresh opportunity for the Christian conscience to turn its necessities to glorious gain. Unemployment has created a new leisured class, which now has opportunity for the first time for the fruitful enjoyment of leisure. To relieve the physical needs of the Unemployed is no adequate Christian solution, though it is obviously a first claim. The genuinely Christian contribution is to utilise the economic necessity for the enhancement of spiritual purposes and the building up of a new social tradition. Some of the most creative social experiments which Christianity has to its credit are those in connexion with unemployment centres.[1] These may still be indefinitely extended, and supply perhaps the best illustration of the way in which, under existing conditions, economic process may be redeemed into the service of personal community.

It is in his capacity as consumer that the individual Christian has the best chance to exercise influence on social policy. Housewives can insist on being supplied with foodstuffs with the particular " mark " which they favour, and can thus stimulate their production. Women of fashion, led by the Queen's example, have almost stopped the destruction of songbirds by refusing to deck themselves in their feathers. They could, if they would, by a similar refusal to buy coats made from the skins of trapped animals, wipe out the horrible cruelties of the fur trade. It is true that under the existing system the purchaser's freedom of choice is restricted to what the producer decides to put on the market. To some extent he must take what he can get. " We are not selling them in that style this year." But there must be some limits to this dictatorship.

In the long run it must rest with the consumer to

---

[1] *Cf.* Miss Cameron's account of the Lincoln experiment in *Civilisation and the Unemployed* (*S.C.M.*).

decide what he is prepared to consume. At the cost, it may be, of some inconvenience and, in extreme cases, of some hardship, he can influence the production of goods and the methods of distribution and supply in such directions as seem to him desirable. A consistent and conscientious employment of their purchasing power by Christian citizens could thus exert an effective control over many departments of industry and commerce and help to organise economic processes for human and spiritual ends. Most of us are on the whole too ready to contract out of this responsibility, blaming everything on " the system." We could at least take steps to ensure that our personal expenditure is productive, and productive of that " wealth towards God " about which the Rich Fool knew so little.

While what has been said applies to commodities, it is still more applicable to services, and most importantly to those services which cater for recreation and publicity. It is the film, the stage and the newspaper which set the tone for the mass of our population ; and no feature in national life is worse than the debauchery of public opinion by irresponsible organs of the Press. Their pernicious influence operates far beyond the frontiers of our own country. Not only does it inflame and embitter international feeling at moments of crisis : it also demoralises the Orient. Our most disreputable Sunday newspaper is said to be the favourite English reading in the native quarters of the Near East. I have seen it myself being hawked in " the land of Sinim."

Against the massed force of these suggestions

Christian preaching might almost seem impotent. The preacher must sometimes feel as he goes to the pulpit, What chance have the ideas for which I stand against those that are being purveyed outside, backed by such an efficient organisation? These misgivings are faithless and despairing. But it is, all the same, true that the strongest and most dangerous opponent of Christianity in public affairs is the exploitation of the popular mind by commercialised propaganda, whether through the Press or through other agencies.

But we cannot serve God and Mammon. We cannot both care for the Kingdom of God and be content that the minds of our fellow-Christians—to say nothing of our fellow-citizens—should be constantly exposed to suggestions which are directly antagonistic to it. We ought to do our best to repel them. This is not a plea for a censorship. Christianity lives in the daylight and can only breathe in the air of free criticism. It must take even the most extreme risk for the sake of moral and intellectual freedom. There is only one completely effective weapon against the dissemination of error, and that is the dissemination of truth. But that is not an argument for encouraging, by the use of our capital or our purchasing power, influences which we exist to discourage.

There are enough Christians in England to guarantee, by concerted action, that at least some undesirable propositions should no longer be paying propositions. We are perplexed to learn that John Newton composed hymns on the deck of a Slaver. Perhaps the appearance on Christians' breakfast

tables of matter which I am not allowed to specify
will be not less perplexing to our successors. But I
take the Press merely as one instance of a principle
which can be widely extended.

3. THE CONSTRUCTIVENESS OF CHRISTIANITY

When all has been said, it remains true that
the essential offer of Christianity to the moralisation
of the new age is the regeneration of character.
During the sixteen years since the Armistice we have
seen goodwill constantly defeated, visions, hopes and
ideals broken, by the sheer recrudescence of evil
overriding the pioneers of faith. This has been
partly due to the madness of fear, penury and humiliation caused by unjust or short-sighted treaties. Nor
can we hope that these demons will be exorcised till
the inflaming causes have been removed : it therefore becomes part of the Christian's duty to work for
a revision of the peace-treaties. But that is not the
whole account of the trouble, and does not alter the
elementary truth that human character is not yet
good enough for the tasks which civilisation lays upon
it. This is where Christianity comes to the rescue.
The Spirit of Christ is the Constructive Spirit, because
it rebuilds character from within and can thus
rebuild its social embodiments.

Communism appeals to the young so strongly
because of its seeming scientific realism. A generation
impatient of uplift and merely vague utopian aspirations is strongly drawn to its realistic programme. It

comports with the steel and concrete architecture characteristic of the twentieth century. It presents itself as a thoroughgoing attempt to deal by material, scientific means with the domination of material forces. It may be cruel, but it has not the impotence of a merely "spiritual" ideology. Indeed, as Earl Russell has shown so brilliantly, the defeat of the pre-war Liberal ideology was due to its inability or reluctance to come to terms with the massive organisation of the new economic techniques. "It is not by pacifist sentiment but by world-wide economic organisation that civilised mankind is to be saved from collective suicide."[1] A religion which is so deeply committed as Christianity to the world of matter should find in this view many congenial elements. And the Christian religion must now prove itself to be no whit less thorough in its realism than the systems which seem antagonistic to it.

We have heard too much about Christian "ideals." Nothing has done more harm to the cause of Christ than flabby talk about the Dreamer of Galilee. For in fact there has never been in history a man so wholly devoid of sentimentalism. He was the greatest Realist ever born. Before His public activity began He faced the lure of religious sentimentality, refusing to dwell in an inner world of dreams unrelated to moral actualities. The siren voice called to Him in vain. He would be true to the facts at all costs—even at the cost of the Cross and Passion. It is not the authentic religion of Jesus which rides away from life on a vague idealism. Thus, in my view, it is

[1] *Freedom and Organisation 1814-1914.*

gravely mistaken to identify the Christian ethic in the crucial problem of peace and war with a negative refusal-to-fight Pacificism—though this does not diminish my reverence for the moral courage of those who support that policy. It is, I think, more consonant with its genius to work for the consummation of peace by the difficult yet morally fruitful method of building up a cooperative security—at whatever price must be paid to win it—as the means to and the expression of community.

At the moment when I was writing this paragraph on a liner in equatorial seas, the principle was being exemplified by the despatch of the international force to secure the integrity of the Saar plebiscite. From it sprang new hope of an understanding between the two great nations across the Rhine.

Nothing that has happened since then, however disappointing or frightening, need weaken our confidence in that principle. Anything that I might write today about the European situation would be out of date before it is printed. But the news each day makes it increasingly clear that a full, equal, mutual guarantee as the expression of a common purpose is the one alternative to annihilation.

The spirit of Christ is the Constructive Spirit. Essentially it reveals its constructiveness in the redemption of character and motive and the redirection of social purpose. St. Paul makes great use of the word " edifying " to express the intrinsic quality of the new life. We have spoilt the word by pious misuse, as when we say that a sermon was dull but edifying. In itself it means " building " or " constructing." And amid the demoralisation and neuroticism of a world which had lost faith in itself because it had lost faith in a living God and a Purpose which gives life significance, it was this inherent moral constructiveness in which the Gospel proved its vitality. The Church " built up itself in love." And love—as perfected personal relationship—is the very meaning of constructive morality. It is therefore the dynamic of the Christian life.

The new age needs a new type of character. The exploiting, feudal type is anachronistic. It served some of the needs of the past century, but has become dangerously incompatible with the social order which has now to be fashioned. For this needs a new kind of courage—not that of the conqueror and the crusader but the essentially Christian form of heroism which dares the adventures of cooperation. What the new age needs is the constructor. Not the knight girt with his sword but the master-builder with his trowel—the artist, the teacher, the healer and the parent, the engineer, the maker and the saint, all who in their several vocations have the touch which conserves life and love—these are the artificers of the new world-order and the symbols of the coming Christianity.

CHAPTER VI

THE FULFILMENT OF THE CHURCH

1. Worship and Work

"HE that is not against us is on our part." " He that is not with me is against me." Superficially regarded the two sayings seem to contradict one another. Yet if taken together as complementary, they express an essential element in the mind of Christ, and in the genius of Christianity. Fanaticism was alien from His temper. When they wanted to call down fire from heaven on villages that refused to receive Him, the Sons of Thunder were witheringly rebuked. When John objected to an exorcism which claimed the authority of the Christian name, the Master repudiated his intolerance : he that is not against us is on our part. The mind of Christ would refuse endorsement to the notion which still lingers in religious circles that no effort is doing God service unless it is set in train by the Church ; so that the League of Nations, for instance, commands but a faint allegiance from some Churchmen because it is not a " Christian " organisation. His faith in God was too strong for that. Upon that depended His fixed resolve to claim in the service of the Kingdom whatever in any way might minister to it.

But not less characteristic of His mind is His sense

of the commanding urgency of the mission entrusted to Him by the Father. An invading host stood on God's soil and by the finger of God He must cast it out. In that war there was no neutrality. Here the decisive issues were set, and here any compromise was perfidy. He that is not with me is against me.

This twofold attitude in the mind of Christ is native to the Christian religion. For this is the genius of Christianity, its divine generosity and tolerance towards all that is good in the surrounding world, *and* its conviction of the unique worth and decisive significance of that which God works in the world through Christ. It is, of course, the practical expression of that faith in God as Creator and Redeemer on which the Christian religion rests. And the Church needs this bi-polar loyalty if it is to fulfil its vocation in the world. The saving knowledge of God through Christ Jesus is more precious than anything else on earth. It is the essential task of the Church to keep that knowledge alive in men's hearts through association in fellowship and worship. The Church is an other-worldly society : if it ceases to be that it is mere lumber. But this indispensable other-worldliness needs to be both balanced and verified by a no less resolute secularity. It cannot live in a spiritual vacuum, any more than our creed can be fenced off from our secular knowledge of nature and history. If it is the business of Theology to interpret the world of our experience, so it is the business of religion to conform our lives to reality. If we attempt to preserve creed and cultus in an artificially protected atmosphere from which the winds of life are excluded they will prove but sterile, exotic plants. Creed and cultus are merely a solemn game unless, on the one hand, they spring spontaneously from a vital communion with God and, on the other, draw life-giving substance from the concrete tasks, claims and interests which are the actual stuff of human activity.

This carries important implications, and gives a distinctive colour to our idea of what membership in the Church means. It implies that politics and economics and the secular concerns of citizenship are essential elements in the life of the Church. The horrible perversion of this idea, to which history bears such depressing witness, must not be allowed to blind us to the truth of it. No doubt it has been terribly abused. The whole scandalous record of the struggle for temporal power is the disastrous consequence. But that sprang from such misunderstanding of the mission and task of the Church as can only be called a " lie in the soul." The Church is not in the world for its own sake but for the salvation of the world. It is not to be ministered unto but to minister. The Christian Church must never use politics as a means to the advancement of its own ends, as an organised institution. It has no ends but those of the Kingdom of God. And it is not an organised polity in the sense that it must defend its own frontiers ; it is the instrument of the Spirit of Christ. If we think of the Church and the world as two rival organised systems, all our thought will start from false premises. The Church is an adventure, not a system. It is that redemption of the social order which God calls forth out of the flux of history. Its mission is to incorporate into Christ ever-increasing elements in the world's life ; or—an alternative form of the same statement—to lose its life in a Christianised world order.

Clericalist methods and ideals we must uncompromisingly reject. History is dark with their betrayals ; and we have seen something of what results from them in Central Europe during the last few years and—nearer to our shores—in Ireland. But the falsity of the clericalist ideal is matched only by that of the suggestion (so dear to the heart of the middle-class Englishman) that religion must be kept out of politics. What is religion in the world for except to redeem man's life to God ? And if all civic interests are excluded, how much is there left of the life of man ? To yield to this dualistic defeatism would leave the Christian life without content, and make of the Church a mere pietist sect. The Church will not be doing Christ's work if it retreats back into the sacristy.

This, however, must not be misinterpreted. It is not my contention that the Church should act corporately and officially in political or economic issues. Even if contemporary conditions made such an idea remotely conceivable it would still be a mistaken demand. The Church cannot behave like the State. It can act only through its saints and prophets, that is to say, through its individual members—as it acted (for example) through Wilberforce to secure the abolition of slavery. It ceases to be a redemptive society unless it is breeding and training Christians who can make this Christian contribution to the moralisation of the world's life. Moreover, any individual Christian who perceives some principle at stake has the right, and indeed the bounden duty, to persuade fellow disciples to share his views and to work up a Christian public opinion.[1] What this amounts to is that the Christian citizen must try to give effect to a Christian policy by exactly the same method as other citizens. But that is not really the point under discussion. What we are here contending for as vital is that the secular tasks of the world are integral elements in the life of the Church, and involved in the service of its altars. Else holiness is a word with no meaning.

For if the life of the Christian consists in being dedicated to the will of God—which is just what holiness means ; and if the content of the divine will is to be sought in all those activities which help to make goodness come true ; then it is the task of the Church to redeem, to sanctify and to direct all worth-while and constructive enterprises. The family, the professions and the Council chamber, the technical skill on which modern life depends, are not merely fields for experiment in which to test our loyalty to the Church. They are themselves the material of Churchmanship.

---

[1] If representative Christian opinion inclines to the views of His Majesty's Opposition rather than those of His Majesty's Government, it is called interference in politics. When recently a number of Christians expressed their wish to sacrifice income for the benefit of the unemployed it was called " an unwarrantable attempt to go behind the back of the House of Commons." People who wrote at the same time to their Member to ask for a reduction of income tax as the first claim on the budgetary surplus were, on the contrary, law-abiding citizens. In any case, what is the House of Commons for ?

That is to say, it is not merely a question of carrying religion out into life amid the temptations of the world. It is a question of doing the world's work and responding to its opportunities with insight cleansed and motive directed by the grace of God through Jesus Christ. Of this grace we are made partakers, and in this faith we are sustained, through the worship and fellowship of the Church.

It is, I think, of the utmost importance to secure this truth in our presentation. For the emphasis in our teaching and suggestion is often false at this particular point, and the evil consequences reach far. The phrase " Church work " tests it like a plumb line. What is meant by doing Church work ? For it is a mistaken answer to this question which has caused the Church to seem irrelevant in the minds of so many young men and women. The world of our time is organised for function : the clergy are thought (whether truly or falsely) to desire to organise it for piety. It is characteristic of this generation to regard technical competence and efficiency as the best form of social contribution. To be good at one's job is the best form of service ; amateurish " uplift " claims no respect. (The falling off of recruits for settlements and similar forms of voluntary philanthropy is due less to desire to get rich quickly or to insensitiveness of social conscience—which is, in fact, far more keen than it used to be—than to a changed approach to the whole issue. One serves the world best in a skilled profession. The well-meaning amateur is an anachronism.) It is inevitable that this attitude should profoundly affect their idea of the

Christian life, and by consequence of the Christian Church. The latter appears to be too much interested in the small activities of a religious coterie and too little in the actual tasks through which its members serve God and man. " Church work " has come to be associated with rather mild parochial organisations which are highly distasteful to many of its members, and appear to have very little relevance to the real business of Christians in the world.

Certainly there is truth in this criticism. People ought not to be led to think that the parish bazaar or the young men's guild are the primary obligations of Church membership. The Christian's duty can never be identified with the way in which people spend their spare time. The primary duty of every Church member is to be doing his job in the world well, for the glory of God and the good of man's estate. It is true, no doubt, that the pastoral work of the Church needs to be more directly related to that consecrated discharge of function in which the " doing of God's will " consists. It may also very likely be true that the Churches are apt to undertake too many inefficient activities, and some which have no obvious connexion with the training of Christians for life and work. Much of the effort expended by the Churches in the way of providing cheap entertainment may, quite probably, be waste of time.

Yet these criticisms may miss the mark. For the Church's concern is with men and women, not as barristers or engineers, but as sinners who may be made saints ; not with what is particular and accidental, but with what is ultimate and universal. The

life is more than meat and the body than raiment;
and the man ought to be more than his profession.
But the ruthless specialisation of the modern world
is tending towards an industrial feudalism which
equates the man with his economic function.   It becomes, therefore, the more imperative that the Church
should provide for its members some opportunities of
a common life in which they may share simply as
Christians, to strengthen their sense of community
in Christ and the family life of God's sons and
daughters.   The local Christian group misses its aim
unless its members can meet as friends, and, so far as
is practicable, know one another.   This friendship
must, however, be centred in the common worship
and the common loyalty ;   else it becomes merely
a hollow heartiness with nothing distinctively Christian about it ;   and this is where we too often fail.

Moreover, what of those members of the Church
whose spiritual lives are devitalised by the humiliation of unemployment ?   One obvious contribution
to this problem is to offer its victims a share in
constructive non-economic activities.   The Church
can do this far more effectively than any other agency
that exists :   it has always work that needs doing.
And the Church will hold the loyalty of its members
in proportion as it demands something from them.
Unless it expects some direct service to the cause
of Christ in the world as one of the conditions of
membership, it becomes merely a club for the pious,
not a means to the redemption of mankind.   The
Church must be a working society.   The parish group
should contain no members who are not responsible

for some job, in accordance with circumstance and opportunity, for the strengthening of its own common life and the further advancement of Christ's cause. It is by doing things that we learn. It is by accepting responsibility for some exacting and sacrificial service that men and women can best be educated in the understanding of Christianity ; and this was the Master's own method. Faith comes to birth out of works. It is through the manifold forms of Christian service which are crying out for more help that Christians can learn the meaning of their own creed and some of the secrets of the Spirit of Christ. It is, too, through the work of Church Councils and the sense of mutual responsibility fostered by this and similar forms of service, whether under the Anglican or other systems, that they can be trained, both in the discipline of self-government in a free state and in the meaning and possibilities of membership in the Universal Church.

All this must be set on the other side. It follows, therefore, that Church work, in the sense of some direct service to the Church of Christ and the cause for which it exists, is an indispensable element in the education of mature Christians. It has come to have an unfortunate connotation. Partly because it is too much associated with tea out of an urn and sausage rolls—things which may be innocent in themselves, but have become unfortunately symbolic of the fatal bias in parish social life towards the second-rate and the shoddy. Partly for much more profound reasons. What has brought the idea into disrepute has been a certain confusion of aim and almost a failure of integrity in the way the Churches have dealt with the whole question. We have allowed ourselves to assume that the organisation of " Church " activities is a desirable end for its own sake, and have not sufficiently clearly related them to the real mission and purpose of the Church.   It is the old fault of introversion.   We have been too much preoccupied with the running of our own machinery.   So we have come to identify Church work with doing something connected with the Church, and have therefore been prone to prolifcrate in an enormous number of small busynesses, without sufficient regard for their value in the making and education of Christians for the service of the Kingdom of God.

The Church is in the world to redeem it.   Therefore all its plans and all its policies must be such as to strengthen it for its proper task and to train men for the Christian vocation in their own callings and professions.   It is not the duty of the average layman to become a kind of amateur parson.   If he has the gifts of the prophet, pastor or teacher he will put them at the Church's disposal.   But the essential task of the Christian is to serve the cause of Christ in his home and the work by which he earns his living, and thus to redeem into the Kingdom of God that given area of the world's life.   That is the true work of the Church, and that is the ministry of all believers.

2. MINISTERS AND MINISTRY

Here we reach one of those principles about which there are widespread misconceptions. One of the weakest points in the Church today is the breach between lay and clerical Christianity. The Englishman is stubbornly anti-clerical and is now, as he has been all through our history, profoundly suspicious of the clergy. This, on the whole, is well for the Church, for a clerical Church is a contradiction in terms. On the other hand, this lack of understanding between ordained and unordained disciples grievously weakens the forces of Christianity. It makes the clergy parsonic and self-conscious ; it leaves the laymen unshepherded and untaught ; and it paralyses united Christian effort. It is probable that much of this tension is due to inadequate appreciation of the true Christian idea of the Ministry. A " sacramental " view of the Ministry is thought by some to involve such pretensions arrogated to itself by a priestly caste as the twentieth century rightly repudiates. Yet the principle of the Christian Ministry is in fact one of the surest tests of God's responsiveness to His people's need—that is, of the truth of the Christian faith in Him. It is thus bound up with all that the Church stands for. It may be some small contribution towards the closing of this dangerous breach if we try to interpret the true place of the Ministry in the life of the Christian society and its redemptive task in the world.

And here as before we approach the question by the opposite road from that which in the past has carried most of the theological traffic. For it has by this time become apparent that this last was leading into a cul-de-sac. Churches have been in conflict for centuries, denying the claims of one another to be true parts of the Church of Christ, because they have assumed that a true Church is defined by the nature of its ministry. But this is to start from a false premiss. Not only does it base the claim of the Church on inductions from historical evidence which is at the least obscure and uncertain : it is also theologically mistaken. For, as the Bishop of Gloucester has insisted,[1] it is the Church that makes the Ministry, not the Ministry that makes the Church. This gives us a more secure criterion. For the nature and function of the Ministry derive from the nature and function of the Church, which in turn derives, as we have already argued, from God's redemptive will for the world as mediated to us by Christ. Hence the whole question about the Ministry runs back to the question, What is the Church for ?

The Church of Christ exists in the world to draw mankind into its faith and fellowship, in order that so the whole life of Man (and perhaps indirectly the life of Nature) may be brought into conformity with God's will. Thus all Christians are called not merely to virtue, but to " holiness." The language of " priesthood " used in the New Testament applies to all members of the Body ; they are to be men sanctified and dedicated to the worship and service of the Father. As " every man is priest in his own household," so every Christian should be priest in his own vocation and sphere of ministry. But a priest " must have something to offer." He cannot dedicate everything in general and offer to God nothing in particular. A man cannot be holy in the

[1] *The Doctrine of the Church and Reunion*, pp. 241–283.

abstract ; he must work out his consecration in the concrete material of the world. And it is because we have sometimes forgotten this that we have succumbed to the fatal tendency to sentimentalise faith and worship, till it becomes emotion without conation—an aspiration without practical content.

If we take the idea of priesthood seriously, its range will extend far beyond the frontier of technically religious activities. It embraces all that a Christian can do, his work, his home life, his leisure, his investments, his expenditure and his politics. All are to be made " otherworldly "—and offered, through Christ, to the Father. That is the priesthood of all believers. For all of us it is " from above " ; it is God's gift and call through Christ Jesus : and it is mediated and sustained by the community of the Holy Spirit. Priesthood is the prerogative of all Christians, and it derives, through the Church, from God. It inheres in membership of the Body. This is what gives the Church its authority to commission some of its members as " ordained " ministers—to the exercise of a specialised function within the priesthood of the whole Body.

Of that priesthood Christ is the Source : it is He who is the ministrant in all sacraments and the giver of all Grace through the Church, which acts—since it must act through somebody—through certain of its own members authorised for this particular task.[1]

---

[1] In the New Testament priesthood is the attribute of Christians as such. Whether it was a true development or a calamity when Old Testament ideas of priesthood began to be applied to the Christian Ministry, is beyond the scope of the present discussion. But it must be remembered that the word " priest," as

But *all* Christian ministry is God-given : the Holy Spirit bestows and enables all forms and expressions of Christian priesthood, and these are meant to include—as we have been arguing—all men's " secular " interests and activities. These are part of the life of the Church. They are as necessary to its fulfilment and to the discharge of its redemptive function as its specifically religious ministries. For if it be true that God was in Christ reconciling the world unto Himself, and if in Christ is the revelation of God's purpose for the whole world, then the Church has not discharged its mission merely in bringing all men to piety. Its task is the reconciliation of all human conduct and purposes with the will of the perfect Source of Goodness. This involves, for example, that our thinking should be reconciled with the truth of God : that confusion, injustice and antagonism should be reconciled with the divine order : that disease and sickness of mind and body should be reconciled with God's laws of health : that the world's politics and economics should be reconciled with the divine purpose in a fellowship of free persons. Thus every attempt to control environment for truly human and spiritual ends is part of God's reconciling work and part of the business of the Christian Church. It is an integral part of Christian ministry. A man's use of his professional skill should be his exercise of his Christian priesthood. When it

applied to one of the orders of the Ministry, is a contraction of the word " presbyter," and therefore does not in itself imply any such priestly prerogatives or functions as may (rightly or wrongly) be held to belong to the office.

is redeemed by the faith of Christ and offered in consecration to the Father, it becomes an essentially
priestly vocation.

This is the grand Pauline conception. Everyone
notes the breadth of St. Paul's vision when he speaks
of the gifts of the exalted Christ, so manifold in
variety of endowment, but alike manifestations of His
presence : "He gave some to be apostles, some
prophets, some evangelists, some pastors and
teachers." But not everyone (I think) has observed
what is implied in this famous passage. The gifts,
however different in expression, are yet all, as we
should say, "ministerial"—the proper endowments
of those who exercise the various forms of religious
ministry. But these are not the whole work of Christ.
They are instruments of an end beyond themselves,
a ministry which all Christians are to exercise :
"for the perfecting of the saints for the work of
ministering, for the building up of the Body of
Christ." [1] The spiritual gifts are bestowed for the
sanctification and redemption of all that Christians
may undertake for the glory of God and the service
of mankind ; and thereby the Church fulfils its
calling. Thus all legitimate "secular" activities are
brought within the scope of the Christian's ministry.
When they are baptised into Christ, they are functions
of the priesthood of all believers.

This perfecting of the saints for the work of ministry
is the responsibility of the Church. It is the concern
of the Body of Christ that its members should so
sanctify their ministry as doctors, parents, engineers

[1] Ephesians iv. 11–13.

and so forth, that through them the manifold life of the world may be reconciled to God's will. And to help one another in these enterprises is the mutual obligation of all believers ; if one member suffers all suffer with it. Yet because the Church primarily exists to be the instrument of the Holy Spirit, its chief and essential responsibility is to guarantee for all its members inward and spiritual participation in God's redemptive gift through Christ Jesus. It must provide for them " means of grace." If it should ever fail to do this it would clearly have ceased to be the Church. It would have become a friendly society, an ethical guild or a social reform club, but would certainly not be the Christian Church. It would not be taking Christ's gift to men. Therefore it is that the one secure title which any body of Christians can show to being a true branch of Christ's Church, is that they care supremely for offering what the Church's first task is to provide. They must show that they know what the Church is for, and are trying faithfully to discharge its function. The obvious sign (or " note ") of that faithfulness is the due provision of members, commissioned in the name of the whole society, to fulfil this specialised form of ministry, on which the very life of the Church depends. The commissioning of ministers for this purpose, to secure the provision, by the whole society and in the name of the whole Body, of the Church's best gift for all its members, irrespective of circumstance or capacity, is decisive and characteristic evidence that the Church is true to its essential function.

The important thing about an ordained Ministry

is that it should be appointed and commissioned by the authority of the whole Body. It must be representative of the Church itself : not merely a number of gifted individuals, but persons "called" by the will of the whole Church to minister Christ's gifts to its members. That is why a duly ordained Ministry is so much more than a matter of mere convenience : it expresses the nature of the Church. You cannot demand that all ordained ministers shall be morally or spiritually worthy ; that would unchurch every Church in Christendom. You can demand that they should be "duly" ordained on the responsibility of the whole Church. The distinction between the Ministry in this sense and the inherent ministry of all Christians is one of function, not Christian quality.

It is obviously true that some laymen are better men than some ordained ministers. The Church may and does make mistakes. It may not always choose the right people. It may not always train them in the best way. But it shows that it means to be faithful to its mission and wills to fulfil its God-given task if it is taking care to provide a Ministry which can speak in its name and act on its behalf. It is the gift of the Church to its members, as the Grace of Christ is God's gift to the Church. It is thus a visible sacrament and symbol of God's responsiveness to His people's need. The importance of episcopal ministries, to those who care greatly for episcopacy, is that they symbolise in a unique way the given-ness of the Ministry to the members through the commission of the whole Body. Episcopal ordination means that wherever you have a congregation led in worship

and sacrament by the curate, there you have, not
Brown, Smith and Robinson, but the Holy Church
Universal.   It does not follow that in the Church of
the future some new development of this principle
may not prove to be practicable or preferable.   We
cannot contend that the whole Church of Christ is
committed irrevocably and for ever to one form of
institutional polity.

There need be nothing " mechanical " or
" magical " in such a conception of the ordained
Ministry.   There is, for example, no branch of Christ's
Church—not even the Roman communion—which
takes a " higher " view of the Ministry or cares more
for its proper provision than does the great Church
of Scotland.   Yet not even the most fanatical Protestant has, to my knowledge, accused Presbyterians of
holding magical views about sacraments.   The authority of the ordained Ministry is the authority of the
Christian fellowship.   It is not that self-constituted
experts dictate to the souls and consciences of their
fellows, which is the sinister connotation of " priest-
craft."   It is that the Christian society, accepting its
mutual obligation for the spiritual care of all members,
commits this leadership and oversight to persons duly
appointed for that purpose.

This is not in the least incompatible with the exercise
by its unordained members of such pastoral or prophetic
ministry or such gifts of prayer or counsel or scholarship
as they may have ability to contribute.   Indeed, it
pre-supposes that background ;   and one of the chief
tasks of the ordained Ministry is the evocation of
spiritual leadership from the lay members of the

society. There is no one in the world more suspicious of " sacerdotalism " than the Protestant Englishman, yet the strange idea which he commonly holds, that Christians cannot rightly pray together unless a parson is present to " offer prayer " for them, is the worst and deadliest form of sacerdotalism. It makes prayer the prerogative of the clergy—which is irreconcilable with Christianity. Would God that all the Lord's people were prophets ! Ministerial priesthood is representative. In its liturgical and official capacity it speaks and acts on the Church's behalf. Not in order that spiritual concerns should be left to the hierophants of a mystery while the people follow their worldly occupations—which is paganism not Christianity—but in order that all members of Christ's fellowship may be gathered within the scope of that action and share in that priestly dedication, making their own vocation and ministry and the stuff and content of their lives a sacrifice, through Christ, to the Father.

A living Church will grow its own ministry, and one obvious test of vitality is the quality of the leadership it throws up. It is clear, moreover, from the New Testament, that the practice of the Church in the earliest days was to give commission and authorisation to those who had already approved themselves as the natural leaders of Christian Groups. These are the " Elders " of St. Paul's Churches—sometimes referred to as Bishops. They were not young men sent to the local Church after receiving a " theological training," as a young doctor starts on a practice. They were

men of standing in that community, already approved
by service and leadership in the life of that Christian
Group. They were men engaged in their own
professions—tentmakers, lawyers, civil servants, etc.,
who had earned the right and title to be commissioned to representative ministerial functions. This
meant that liturgical and pastoral leadership had its
roots deep in the common life, and sprang out of
intimate association with the secular activities of the
Group. Thus it represented the life of the Church,
both on behalf of its members and towards them, in
a most actual and significant way. Roland Allen has
rightly insisted on the wide difference between this
system and that which has come to obtain in the
modern Churches. And it is, I think, important to
recognise that in the transition to the modern system—
however inevitable it has been in practice—some vital
Christian values have been obscured.

I am not now discussing the question whether the
traditional " threefold Ministry "—which may or
may not be discovered in Scripture—is the necessary
or the best form. Nor are we concerned, at the
moment, with the contribution of non-episcopal
Ministries to the united Church of the future. The
point which I am trying to make now is independent
of these delicate questions. Whatever a man's views
on these issues, and whatever his attitude to Episcopacy, he can hold that something important has been
lost in the evolution of the Ministry from its primitive
form to the twentieth century. From the standpoint
of my present contention all the Churches are in the
same boat—except the Friends, who have no ordained

ministers. In what follows, I seek to be quite realistic. I am not suggesting wild revolution. Accepting the system which we have inherited, I suggest only such modifications as will make the Ministries, as at present constituted, more genuinely sacramental of the fundamental Christian idea. This, so far as concerns the Church of England, involves an attempted re-presentation of the case for so-called " voluntary " clergy. It is stated in terms of Anglican precedent. But the principle, *mutatis mutandis*, would be equally applicable in the other Churches.

The case appears to have been misunderstood. It seems to have been presented to Lambeth chiefly in terms of an improvised expedient to remedy the shortage of ordained men, especially in the Dominions and in the Mission-field. But that is in fact its least important aspect. Those of us who attach great importance to it do so, not on grounds of expediency, but of ultimate Christian and sacramental principle. In the Church of England as organised at present— and the same is broadly true of most other Churches —nobody can be ordained to the Ministry unless he has first agreed to take payment for it, *i.e.*, to make it a " profession." Even if he wishes to give his services freely he must nevertheless execute an agreement to accept a " peppercorn " stipend. So profoundly has professionalisation affected our ideas of the Ministry. For reasons which reach far back into past history ministerial life is regarded as a profession, inconsistent with any secular occupation, other than farming or teaching school or sitting in an office in Church House—exceptions which are not self-explanatory.   Unless a man is prepared to accept that, the Church is not prepared to ordain him.

Now this system is partly bound up with questions of discipline and administration, which makes Bishops reluctant to modify it ; partly also, and far more importantly, with the idea that it serves to safeguard the " sacred calling " of the ordained minister against the contaminations of worldliness.   But that is false, both in principle and in practice.   A sacramental conception of the Ministry is no more necessarily bound up with a whole-time stipendiary profession than it is with the curious passion of Anglican dignitaries for walking about the streets of our cities in the riding habit of the eighteenth century.   The equation of " sacred " with " non-secular " is not supported by Christian thinking.   Moreover, to make the Ministry a profession is to involve it in all those calculations of stipend, status and social privilege from which the system aims at exempting it.   That is not in itself an objection against it, for any system will have its peculiar temptations.   But it does disprove the claim that is sometimes made for it, to be a safeguard against worldly motives.

The effective defence of the present system is empirical rather than *a priori*.   It is that the task is so exacting, and demands so much time and concentration, both intellectual and spiritual, as to be incompatible with other activities—schoolmastering and farming always excepted.   Now this is true—or, if it is not, it ought to be—as the ministerial system is worked at present.   If what we mean by the Ministry is the Rectors and Curates of parishes, the assertion is not seriously disputable. But *is* this necessarily what we mean ? That is indeed the real point at issue. Can we not conceive an ordained Ministry other than that of Rectors and Curates ?

As we have already observed, the trend of events seems to be leading us towards a kind of industrialised feudalism in which everybody will have his place, from which no change or escape can be expected, in a graded, hierarchised community. Each year we are reverting more closely to Plato's ideal of a caste polity ; and experiments both in Europe and the United States all seem to confirm this prediction.[1] But the Christian society is not at all likely to remain unaffected by this tendency. Indeed, it is being affected already. The demand made on the Ministry of the Church is not only far more exacting, but it is also a great deal more specialised than it was in 1835, and this pressure is likely to become stronger. The kind, friendly, amateurish parson is already becoming an anachronism. The Ministry demands, more and more, a technical and specialised training, and its functions are becoming increasingly specialist.

From one point of view, this is all to the good. It means that in future the Ministry of the Church must be manned by very highly selected men, and the standard of qualification and training will have to be fixed far higher than it is now. It is probable that the task of the *Parochus* will, in future, be more and more concentrated on three highly specialised services—on teaching, on leadership in prayer and worship, and on the

---

[1] *Cf.* the ghastly forecast of it by Mr. Aldous Huxley in *Brave New World*.

skilled, expert " cure of souls." These are the proper ministerial functions. It will never, of course, work out in practice—nor would it on the whole be desirable —that all the administrative and public work which at present falls to the rector of a big parish should be entirely removed from his shoulders. The general direction of the life of the group must inevitably be vested in him, and he must be, so far as possible, its *persona* in all that concerns Christ's cause in the district. But his functions will be increasingly " religious," and much that is at present expected of him will remain undone or be done by others.

This is to be welcomed as, on the whole, " a good thing." It has been the strength of the Anglican tradition that its clergy, however amateurish, have always been intimately in touch with the main stream of national thought and life. The English suspicion of a clerical caste and its dislike of " seminary train- ing " is indeed a thoroughly wholesome prejudice. Yet a man must know how to do his job and—in the world into which we are moving—must stick to the job which he knows how to do. Religious teaching, leadership in worship and the cure of souls are highly skilled trades. All of them demand, for their due discharge, liberal education and wide sympathies. To urge that these are the true tasks of the Ministry is not a plea to reverse our tradition and return to the ordination of chantry-priests. It is, indeed, precisely the contrary.

Yet this specialisation of function, which is woven into the pattern of the coming age, must carry with it peculiar dangers. It can hardly fail to increase that tendency to the departmentalising of life, with the spiritual sterility that results from it, which has been already described and deplored. More than ever the Church will be needed to rescue men from this narrowing process and restore to life unity and significance. Yet it will only be with great difficulty and by taking deliberate precautions that the Church itself can resist this pressure. All the forces to which it will be exposed will be driving it back inwards upon itself. Preoccupied with its own preservation, and cut off from fructifying contact with the currents of life in the world around it, the Church will then be in grave danger of spiritual anæmia and atrophy. Nor can its Ministry hope to be immune. If religion itself becomes a specialisation, the specialist concerns of the Ministry cannot fail to be more and more limited to technical and ecclesiological interests. This is, indeed, already becoming noticeable. The Church should surely take deliberate steps to counteract this disastrous rift between religion and the life of the world.

One aim of this volume, and of its predecessor, is an attempt to forestall this false development by exploring its theological implications. But in practice we could do much to resist it by the ordination of " voluntary " clergy. What is really important about this suggestion is not the alleviation which it might offer to the problem of staffing the parishes. That could be solved far more effectively by a courageous redistribution of human and material resources. It is rather that it would help to exhibit in a truly sacramental expression the essential principle of the

Christian Ministry. It would demonstrate that the Ministry of the Church is potentially exercised by all its members. It would make it clear that the ordained Ministry is sustained by, as it is meant to " perfect," that essential priesthood of all believers which embraces every legitimate vocation. It would thus help to save Christianity from becoming a caricature of itself as something that people do after working hours.

In principle, the suggestion is this, that side by side with the whole-time Ministry the Church should confer ministerial commission on a limited number of its members, Christians of standing in their own group and accredited in their own professions. These while they continued to exercise their own forms of vocation and ministry, would be ordained to administer the sacraments or to preach and teach, according to their ability, supporting themselves by their own professional work. These " non-stipendiary " ministers would thus be almost exactly analogous to the presbyters of the first century. Where there was no *parochus* available, as in the Bush or in outlying Missions, or in emergency in a home parish, they would act as the priests of the communities. In the more settled conditions of English life they would normally serve under the parish priest, and in any case under Episcopal supervision. It is urged that thus, in the younger Churches, isolated groups of Christ's people could meet for the Eucharist on the first day of the week, under their own duly ordained President, instead of waiting six or twelve months for a visiting priest from some distant centre. The latter, as Roland Allen rightly insisted, is a travesty of the Church's intention.

For England, where circumstances are so different, the suggestion is based on quite different grounds. It is true that if the experiment were successful it would, in time, contribute materially to the solution of many difficult questions, not least those of parochial finance, and save many clergy from breaking down. But the real strength of the case is one of principle. It is the desire to exhibit the Ministry as the consecration and focus of the ministry of the whole Christian body in the normal activities of life. This is, I believe, of first-class importance if the life of the Church is to be strong and healthy. What would it not mean to the Christian Group if the ministrant of God's gift for the sanctification of its Christian ministry were one who was actually sharing in the tasks and temptations of " secular " daily life, and were looked up to as its natural leader in the life of Christian citizenship and service ? Nor can one think of any experiment which, while preserving the Christian emphasis on the " given-ness " of the means of Grace, as symbolised by a duly ordained Ministry, would do so much to safeguard the Church against the dominance of the clerical mind. It would help very effectively to demonstrate the sacramental character of the Church and the priestly vocation of the Christian life. It is on these essentially catholic grounds that the suggestion ought to be brought forward.

So far as regards the Church overseas, the case for a non-stipendiary Ministry was tentatively accepted at

Lambeth. But it was endorsed only as an expedient justified by exceptional circumstances, and was by implication if not in words rejected so far as concerns the Home Church.[1] The case had not, perhaps, been brought forward quite in the light in which it is here presented as a matter of high sacramental principle ; and it is to be hoped that it may be reconsidered. The suggestion violates no catholic principle : it involves merely a change in accepted custom and a partial reversion to apostolic practice. Nobody who has given much thought to it will be blind to those administrative difficulties which, inevitably and quite rightly, count for so much in the judgment of the Episcopate. But no reckless changes are asked for. A controlled experiment on a small scale might be tried out in a few chosen centres where the conditions are obviously favourable ; in University towns, for example. The ordained tutor in a college, taking his share in its life and teaching and also serving as Minister and Chaplain, is in an exceptionally strong position. All that the present proposal really asks for is a certain extension and application of this already existing arrangement. If the experiment seemed to be justified, it could then be extended on an enlarged scale. It might be, in time, that large business houses could thus be provided with their own Minister, who was in fact one of their own staff. The parochial system in England was evolved in different social conditions from those which prevail in the twentieth century, and perhaps it needs now

[1] *Report of Lambeth Conference*, 1930, Resolution 65 and Report, pp. 175-177.

to be supplemented by an ordained Ministry of a new kind.

If the experiment were to secure approval, the system could then be established, under due safeguards, in the large parishes. This would, in time, diminish considerably the number of young men of twenty-three who were ordained straight from their colleges to a professional or whole-time Ministry. There would probably be nothing but gain in this. It would automatically force up the standard. It would widen the basis of the ordained Ministry. It would provide for poverty-stricken parishes. And it would evoke from unordained members—through the Bridge-Ministry of the non-stipendiaries—new gifts of pastoral and prophetic ministry for the " edifying " of the whole Body.

An effective retort is, of course, open. It may be replied that the whole suggestion cuts across the admitted principle of specialised function in the modern world. The answer is that this is the strength of it. We cannot allow spiritual leadership to fall entirely into the hands of " specialists." You can be an expert in Christianity without being a specialist in " religion." That is the principle which we wish to vindicate. It is urged, again, that the non-stipendiaries would not greatly assist the *parochus*, since the need in the great parishes is not so much provision for " taking services " as the pastoral care of vast populations. But a vast amount of work is already done by accredited unordained leaders in preaching, teaching, pastoral visitation and the care and guidance of adolescents ; and this devoted, sacrificial work is the strength of the Church's life in the parishes. Such persons would not cease from these ministries nor begin to perform them with less skill if they were ordained to the priesthood. But that act would give recognition to the pastoral ministry which they are discharging.

The proposal known as the Permanent Diaconate, which is sometimes advanced by way of alternative, would quite fail to supply what is needed. For the right to celebrate at the Eucharist is the essential point of the whole suggestion. If a person selected for this new type of Ministry had a gift for preaching or teaching, the Church, naturally, would desire to use it. But in fact it does this at present, and some of its most gifted and influential lay members give devoted service. This does not necessitate ordination. What I mean is something entirely different from the ordination of Lay Readers. The real point is that some members of the Church, foremost in responsibility for the world's work, should be authorised to administer the Eucharist, and thus to consecrate in ordained Ministry the ministry of all Christian people. That means ordination to priesthood ; and nothing less would have any real value. What matters here is simply the authorisation to act in the Church's name and behalf. And this in fact completely invalidates the whole idea of a " permanent diaconate."

The actual distribution of Holy Communion demands no qualifications whatever beyond clean hands and (if possible) a pure heart. What is crucial is the authority to do this, and all that is implied in conferring it. But preaching and teaching in the name of the Church demand both qualifications and training. It is not suggested that all non-stipendiaries would be as well equipped in theology or in the technique of Ministerial work as the " professional " or whole-time Ministers. Their status in the Christian society would rest on other and different qualifications ; and in virtue of these they would be commissioned to represent the ministering community and discharge its chief Ministerial function. It is obvious that, under oversea conditions, the diaconate would not serve the purpose : for the people would still be left without sacraments (unless, indeed, we accept the position that " in the absence of the priest " the deacon may act as his representative, as he does now in administering Baptism). Under English conditions nothing much would be gained by admitting Vice-chancellors into deacon's orders. They had much better stay as they are.

The same considerations seem to apply to the ordination of women to the Ministry. The diaconate does not serve the purpose ; indeed it limits the range of a woman's ministry. Under the regulations at present in force she can do more as an unordained member than she can when she has been ordained deaconess. In any case a " representative " priesthood which excludes half mankind from its membership can only claim to be representative in a very peculiar theological sense. The claim of the women is logically unanswerable. I have little doubt that within the present century—though not at all probably in my lifetime—the Church will have

been guided to concede it.   And it is surely, within
the wider scheme of a new non-stipendiary priesthood,
supplemental to the existing Ministry, that the first
experiments in this direction could be authorised most
hopefully.

3. BODY OF CHRIST

The Ministry is organic to the whole Body.   One
reason for the sub-Christian theories by which it
has sometimes been overlaid is, I think, failure to
appreciate what the phrase, the Body of Christ, means.
Most of us leave it as a merely pious metaphor.   We
do to a small extent understand our debt to the
Christian group which has nurtured us, but have
hardly begun to grasp what is entailed in membership
in a universal community.   We use the phrase quite
vaguely and loosely, as we speak of " a large body of
Englishmen," of the aggregate of individual Christians.
But that is not its use in the New Testament.   There,
it means the Christian society as the instrument of
Christ in the world and the outward manifestation
of His Spirit, the visible habitation in which He
dwells.   It means the Church as a sacramental reality,
not merely a fortuitous collection or association of
believers.   Nor is it an idealised Church which is thus
described by St. Paul.   It is the actual visible society
with all its sins, negligences and ignorances amid the
resistances of history and the frustrations of the time
process, which is the organ of the divine purpose.   It
is compact of persons and things, not of spiritual
aspirations.   It is an outward and visible sacrament

of Christ's redemption in the life of the world. However inadequate, there is no other. The facile theory of a Church invisible, by contrast with the empirical Church of history, can find no support in the New Testament.

Unfortunately, however, those Christians who have grasped St. Paul's meaning most firmly have been too prone to pervert the idea in the sense of a closed institutional system through which alone Grace is made available and outside which there is no salvation. And notoriously this has borne fruit in a temper, an outlook and an attitude which has brought shame upon the name of Christ. After all, whatever we mean by " body " at least it exists to express a spirit, not to be opaque to its purposes. It is a mind and purpose in action. But therefore it is never a static system ; it is something which is alive and developing.

A body is not a fixed quantity. It is no mere aggregate of substances, nor is it merely the envelope of a spirit. It is the instrument of a life-purpose. It derives its identity and continuity not from the materials which compose it—for these are in constant process of metabolism—nor from the patterns into which it is organised—for it may yet persist in a changed pattern ; but from the purpose by which it is informed. It is constantly fashioned and refashioned out of the changing materials of environment. Ever new substances and energies are incorporated into a body as the vehicle of the life which informs it. This is true of a body at any organic level. It is the organisation of life-purpose establishing itself in the world. On the human level it is more. We

find man constantly increasing the range of his response
to environment—when he ceases to do this he is dead.
And whatever becomes the instrument of the man—
the machinery through which he exerts his will, his
home, his work, his possessions and his friendships—
is thereby in a true sense incorporated into that
particular pattern of energy, informed and directed
by his spirit and made organic to his life-purpose,
which is what we mean by his body. Thus a body
is not merely a system. It is something always in
process of becoming as purpose develops in range and
concentration and embodies itself creatively in the
world.

This is of the utmost significance. For it means
that the Church as the Body of Christ is itself in
process of becoming and is never a static institutional
system. If, as St. Paul daringly suggested, Christ
Himself is " coming to his fulfilment "[1] then the Body
of Christ is never a constant term. It, too, is coming
to its fulfilment, as more and more elements in the
world's life are redeemed from the dominion of
worldliness and incorporated into the Church, thus
being made organic to God's will and embodiments
of Christ's Spirit. Thus the Church is always unfinished, and is yet to be realised on earth. To
profess belief in the Holy Catholic Church is not to
assert that any of the existing Churches is in itself
the true Church of Christ or exclusively the home of
salvation. It is to pledge a faith and a loyalty. We
believe in our own Churches and traditions in so far
as they serve the ends of the one true Church universal,

---

[1] Ephesians i. 23.

which in sundry portions and divers manners seeks incarnation in the world.

But the claim to belong to the true Church is a vow to work and pray for its fulfilment. It involves an inclusive, not an exclusive temper, the tolerance of a truly Catholic spirit, not that sectarian complacency with which the word is too frequently identified. Evangelism and missionary mindedness are among the obvious tests of " catholicity." Those who most believe in the Church should surely be those who desire most eagerly the ingathering of all mankind into the faith and fellowship of the Gospel. Those whose gratitude is most awakened for the grace given to them through their own Church ought to be conspicuous in this ambition. No one Church in its isolation can claim the fullness of Christian experience. We do not even know what the Church is till it has become universal. It is as yet but a foretaste and a promise.

Thus the fellowship of Christ's Church, though here and now real and actual, is yet always to be fulfilled. Its present reality is instrumental to a still unrealised fruition ; and that both intensively and extensively. It must be remembered, in this connexion, that the Christian Church is not meant to be a society of like-minded persons akin to a club or a political party. It entails a much more exacting loyalty. For it is an adventure of gathering into unity all sorts and conditions of men and women, differing in capacity and temperament, in social inheritance, outlook and character. As Bishop Gore used frequently to exclaim " ecclesiastical " ought to mean " brotherly." Hence the achievement of Christian fellowship is and always must be far harder than to get a unanimous vote at a party meeting. And it is more worth while to achieve. A Church in which everybody thinks alike is a sub-Christian and commonplace ideal. There can be no standardised Christian unity. There are no doubt, at least in the Church of England, and that at both ends of the theological spectrum, people whose ideal of Christianity is that all Christians should share their point of view. But it is hard to believe that this marches either with the purpose of God in history or with the true nature of Christian fellowship. The richest unity lives in variety ; and it is only this recognition which can support the claim of the Church to be the focus of human community.

To remember this helps to explain, even though it does not condone or justify, the ignominious contro-versies among Christians. But it also suggests the constructive remedy. If any Church or denomination becomes merely monochrome in complexion, then any group in it who feel strongly about some aspect of Christian experience to which, in their view, it fails to do justice, are driven to one of two false reactions. They must either attempt to " capture " that Church for their own particular interpretation, or they must break away as dissenters. Both actions are equally sectarian, even though in the past the latter course has sometimes been imposed upon Christians by the intolerance of the parent bodies. The faith of a living Church must be strong enough not merely to tolerate but to encourage varieties of emphasis and expression. And we are moving into a new climate, in which

differences of interpretation are seen to be not contradictory but diverse manifestations of the one
Spirit. We have nearly advanced, after two thousand
years, to the position St. Paul took for granted.

It is told of a well-known Japanese Christian that,
speaking in England about Christian unity, whenever
he meant to refer to denominations he said, by a slip
in his English, " damnations." Will anyone say he
was wholly wrong? A man can learn the meaning
of Christian fellowship only within some actual
Christian society. If he wants to belong to the true
Church he must belong to one of the Churches,
sharing its life, its worship and its traditions. In the
world that we mortals know an ideal which is unem-
bodied remains ghost-like and insubstantial ; an
unparticularised universal never enters the field of
reality. It is the Confessions and Denominations,
the given, empirical Churches that are, which must
be regarded as instruments of the Holy Church
Universal. And the richer and deeper their own
common life the more effective instruments they can
be. Under the conditions imposed upon us by
history, faithfulness to his own denomination is
normally part of a Christian's duty. But denominations may be damnations and partake of the nature
of deadly sin, if they allow themselves to become
sectarian.

There can be one justification only for continued
denominational loyalties. It is that the characteristic forms of experience and interpretation to
which, through its historical legacy, a given denomination bears witness are regarded as gifts held in trust

for the building up of the Body of Christ. None of us is directly responsible for the limiting conditions which we inherit. But we are responsible for transcending them. There is a right and a wrong way of attempting it. The wrong way is that of detached indifference to all denominational differences and a scaling down of their living variety to an abstract common denominator. This watery undenominationalism would find few supporters today. The right way is interdenominational—to cherish that which is most distinctive in the tradition which has been bequeathed to us, not with a sectarian self-sufficiency but as a contribution to the Great Church.

Thus convinced and whole-hearted membership in any of the Churches of Christendom cannot but be fragmentary and incomplete. It must always be pointing beyond itself to the Church in which it will find fulfilment. They without us cannot be made perfect. The " end " of all the existing Churches is incorporation into the true Church, and their strength —perhaps even their survival—will depend on the conviction and courage with which they offer themselves to this destiny. The insular policy is but group-suicide. Thus if they would establish their claim to be true branches of the Church, two things are demanded of the Churches. First, such a passionate concern for the evangelisation of mankind as that the Church may become catholic ; and secondly, such cooperation in the carrying out of that enterprise as that the Church may be made one.

Notoriously one of the fatal weaknesses in the Christian mission throughout the world lies in our

P

separations and divisions. It is, as we saw in the first chapter (pp. 30-34), when the Churches are face to face with heathenism that these divisions become most intolerable and at the same time least significant. The stream of history has flowed far since the days when the Churches became divided. It is now scarcely possible to maintain that the lines of denominational demarcation correspond with spiritual reality. True, that each of the separated Churches came into being in order to bear witness to some one aspect of the whole faith. True, as we have already emphasised, that each of these various traditions has its place, of right, in the Universal Church and must not be abandoned or overwhelmed in a standardised Christianity. But much that was in the past distinctive has now become part of the common legacy. Divisions that were, at the time, inspired by positive and constructive convictions are now becoming negative and unreal. They no longer correspond with the facts. (There is, for example, a far wider variety within the unity of the Anglican Church than there is between the two wings of that Church and the Romans and Free Churchmen respectively.) Beyond all question these divisions are obstacles to the redemption of the world. How much can it matter in the sight of God whether one or another denomination preserves its independent existence, compared with the question whether Asia is won for the allegiance of Christ, or whether conflicting and terror-stricken nations are gathered into the fellowship of the Church in a true spiritual community? And if the effort to keep alive Churches hinders the conversion of the world and the coming of the Church universal, we cannot doubt which is the prior claim. How many of the Churches now separated stand for anything positive enough or sufficiently valuable and distinctive to justify further prolongation of a separation that may have been inevitable, but is now a hindrance to their vocation ? Each must answer according to conscience. But however unique and precious the witness committed to any one of the Churches, it can be given more, not less, fruitfully as an element in the united witness of a Church truly one and truly catholic. Unless the seed is willing to die " it abideth by itself alone." It may pass through " death " into newness of life within a more glorious community in which it is not absorbed but fulfilled.

" The idea of a universal church," wrote Dr. Inge in his farewell message, " is as obsolete and chimerical as that of a universal empire." [1] That seems to depend on what we mean by it. If it means an institutional system with a uniform centralised government in one massive world-wide organisation like " the ghost of the Roman Empire sitting crowned upon the grave thereof," I should be in entire agreement. Even if we thought it desirable, the attitude of the Roman communion makes such an idea inconceivable in any future that we can envisage. Nor do I think it even desirable. The history both of the Church and the Empire is a conclusive warning against it. But the phrase need not necessarily mean this. The commonwealth of British peoples and the

[1] *Vale*, p. 102.

world-wide Anglican communion illustrate a different
interpretation and point the way to a more hopeful
method. Uniformity is a false ideal. In the united
Church of the future there must be—and it is almost
true to say that there are now in the Anglican communion—as many varieties in the forms of worship
and of local government and administration as there
are differences of temperament and of social and
racial inheritance. The constituent groups will be
one Church not only in theory, but in fact, through
mutual recognition of Ministries and full reciprocity
of communion. Differences will not mean divisions.

No one who thinks realistically is at all likely to
underestimate the difficulties which still block the
road. Yet unity is the demand of faith for those who
believe in the True Church, as they believe in Justice,
Peace and Freedom, because it is held within the
Divine Purpose, and dedicate their lives to its
realisation.

But the Church is a Body, not an idea. We must
never allow ourselves to forget that no mere extension
of membership, nor even the achievement of reunion,
is an adequate aim for believers in the Church. We
must apprehend the depth and height of the Great
Church as well as its length and breadth. It must pene-
trate and not merely increase. That the Church
should cover the earth's surface with an organisation
of Christians is not enough. Its task is to redeem
the world's life. Our Lord was relentless about people
who compass sea and land to make proselytes for the
sake of a self-contained institution. The less the
Church thinks about itself, and the greater its concern

for the world which it is God's purpose to redeem, the more will it be true to its vocation. It must be ambitious to reclaim those great tracts of secular civilisation which are still unredeemed territory, yet to be won back into the Kingdom of God. It will study not only to make more Christians, but so to christen their day-by-day activities in their secular groupings and associations—whether social, political or economic—that men may come " to recognise Christ as the true centre of their fellowships." [1] Its task is to reconcile to God, through the faith and work of its members, the manifold functions of life in time as the vehicle of the life eternal. It is thus that the true Church comes to be. For this is to fashion in history that Body in which the living Christ is incarnate, and God's reconciling purpose verified. So the Father's will shall be done, on earth as it is in heaven, and Christ shall be exalted in victory.

[1] The phrase comes from F. D. Maurice. In my article in *Christianity and the Crisis* I attributed it wrongly to Wesley.

INDEX

231

PRINTED IN GREAT BRITAIN BY THE WHITEFRIARS PRESS LTD
LONDON AND TONBRIDGE